The Burning Question

Also by Ruth Brandon

NON-FICTION

Singer and the Sewing Machine, a Capitalist Romance
The Dollar Princesses
The Spiritualists

FICTION

Left, Right and Centre
Out of Body, Out of Mind

The Burning Question

The anti-nuclear movement since 1945

Ruth Brandon

HEINEMANN : LONDON

William Heinemann Ltd
10 Upper Grosvenor Street, London W1X 9PA
LONDON MELBOURNE JOHANNESBURG AUCKLAND

First published in Great Britain 1987
Copyright © Ruth Brandon 1987

British Library Cataloguing in Publication Data

Brandon, Ruth
  The burning question : the anti-nuclear
  movement since 1945.
  1. Anti-nuclear movement–History
  I. Title
  327.1'74   JX1974.7

ISBN 0 434 08534 0

Photoset by Deltatype Ltd., Ellesmere Port
Printed and bound in Great Britain by
Mackays of Chatham

For Anne, Dee, Jane and Kaye

'Will you walk a little faster?' said a whiting to a snail,
'There's a porpoise close behind us, and he's treading on my tail.'
See how eagerly the lobsters and the turtles all advance!
They are waiting on the shingle – will you come and join the dance?
Will you, won't you, will you, won't you, will you join the dance?
Will you, won't you, will you, won't you, won't you join the dance?

Lewis Carroll
Alice's Adventures in Wonderland

Contents

Preface   ix

1   A Failed Infanticide   1
2   Amateurs and Professionals   10
3   Under the Counter   21
4   Protest   30
5   CND   37
6   On the March   46
7   Fallout   54
8   The Sixties   60
9   Waging Peace   70
10   Atoms for Peace   81
11   Protest Resurfaces   93
12   America and the Freeze   103
13   Triggerpoints   109
14   Secrets   118
15   Why Do People Hate the Peace Movement?   133
16   Religious War and Religious Peace   139
     Conclusion   152
     Notes   156
     Select Bibliography   165
     Index   169

Preface

So much happens every day in politics that it is often hard to recall the timing or importance of any single incident or party. But in this over-busy scene it is remarkable how the single-issue campaigns remain memorable. Anti-slavery, the Gandhian movement against Colonial rule, Black civil rights, anti-Vietnam, anti-apartheid – these are all campaigns which stirred people's imagination and emotions and brought them, perhaps for the first and only time, into active politics.

The campaign to abolish nuclear weapons has, ever since the use of the atom bomb against Japan, been one of the most active of these movements. It flourishes in both hemispheres and on both sides of the Iron Curtain (though this book deals mostly with its activities in the West). This spread is hardly surprising, since it is generally acknow-ledged that nuclear weapons endanger the whole world. But because of the sporadic and intense nature of this activism, it is very hard to get any sense of the movement as an historical whole. To participate in a big political demonstration, which is for many people their main point of contact with the movement, is an extraordinary, emotional and consuming experience. Single-issue politics consists largely of a succession of such moments, each of them concentrating on the future, the next big push which may achieve the goal. To stand back and place them within a coherent framework is hard: the temptation is always to immerse oneself in the politics of the present, not the past.

But the peace movement repays study. Its story is interesting both in itself and for the light it throws on aspects of the political scene: the

Cold War, the way politics works in different places, and some of the more curious politico-psychological traits of the post-war era.

The amount of material available on this subject is vast and growing, and any book that tried to be in any way exhaustive would be a very long one. This is a rather short book: obviously the choices I have made as to what to include have been somewhat arbitrary. What I have tried to do is to pick out salient moments and events, and through them to follow certain themes. Among these are: the growing awareness of scientists of the part they play in modern warfare, and their reactions to this. The different methods used by politicians and the military to defuse unwelcome comment. Connected with this, the enormous discrepancies between what is said and what is done (or, to put it less politely, the use of lies). On another level, the perhaps unrecognised discrepancies between what is said and what is really meant: the topic of nuclear weapons has a unique propensity to defeat logic and rationality in argument and replace them with fury, fear and prejudice. Then, with its history of rebirth in different places and at different times, the peace movement can provide insights into the mechanisms that seem to trigger public concern at a particular moment, and also into the way single-issue politics works in different political systems.

More generally, this is a story about the deep irrationality of politics and the curious pervasiveness of hope.

Acknowledgements

A great many people have helped me in the preparation of this book, and I should like to thank them all. In particular I am grateful to: Francis Aprahamian, Pat Bateson, Stewart Britten, Owen Greene, John Humphrey, Nick Humphrey, Mike Pentz, Martin Rees, and – as always – Philip Steadman. I need hardly add that they do not necessarily agree with what I have to say. Any mistakes are entirely my own.

1

A Failed Infanticide: the bomb is born and used

'I sometimes read books about the future in which the scientist plays the part of the magician in the old fairy tales. In our grandfathers' time the scientist was a good magician. He was going to make machines to do all our work for us without producing unemployment. Air transport was to usher in an era of universal peace; and so on.

'Today bad magicians are more fashionable. Mr Wells tells us of new and worse poison gases, Mr Stapleton of synthetic disease germs, and Mr Michael Arlen of explosives far more powerful than anything that exists today.

'Fortunately these stories are as improbable as the others. . .'
– J.B.S. Haldane, 'What Next In Science?' from Keeping Cool, *1940.*

It is a truism that military needs have often prompted great scientific advances. Of course this does not mean that scientists are a particularly bloodthirsty group; rather, scientific advance requires both a framework within which problems may be formulated and, usually, funding to answer the new questions raised. The military are in a unique position to provide both these requisites.

By the 1930s it was becoming clear to some scientists that science and war were becoming so bound up, and that the science of war was now so complex, that scientists could no longer leave the conduct and communication of what scientific progress implied to the politicians. Groups such as the Cambridge Scientists' Anti-War Group took it upon themselves to point out to the public how woefully the British government was under-preparing for possible enemy attack (one of the group's luminaries, J. B. S. Haldane, wrote a whole book on A.R.P. – Air Raid Precautions). This did not endear them to the authorities; nevertheless, many of their suggestions were taken up, and when war came members of the group such as Haldane and J.D. Bernal became trusted government advisers.

Of the most closely kept scientific secret on the Allied side, however, Haldane and Bernal had not an inkling. Like almost everyone else, they dismissed the actual achievement of atomic explosive energy as a pipe-dream for the far distant future, and went on so dismissing it even when work on the bomb had actually begun. This misapprehension was due to the timing of the key discovery – that of the fissionable nature of uranium, which was not hit upon by Otto Hahn until December 1938. Hahn communicated it to his erstwhile collaborator, Lise Meitner, now exiled in Stockholm, who told her nephew, Otto Frisch, who in turn discussed it with his mentor, the great Danish physicist Niels Bohr, in January 1939. Bohr immediately realised what Hahn's discovery meant; but by then the world situation was such that these were no longer matters for open discussion. They were to remain deeply secret until after the war ended, when (as we shall see) the whole question of this secrecy, its feasibility and whether or not it was desirable, was to become central to the debate which began then and which has been raging ever since as to what is to be done about nuclear weapons. Meanwhile even the best-informed of those outside the nuclear charmed circle based their projections of what was likely to happen in the next war on their knowledge of what had happened in the last – a state of affairs which, despite everything, still obtains to a surprisingly large extent.

Of course Hahn did not make his historic discovery in an intellectual vacuum. The problems of atomic structure, and the possibility of fission, had been at the front of every physicist's mind ever since Marie Curie discovered, in 1898, that radiation was an atomic property. In 1914 H. G. Wells published a novel, *The World Set Free*, in which an atomic war takes place due to a physicist discovering how the energy locked up in the nucleus of the atom can be

2

released as the result of a chain reaction. In the novel this discovery takes place in 1933. The novel was not successful, but in 1932, after Wells had become famous, a German translation of it was published in Berlin, where it was read with avid interest by a young physicist named Leo Szilard. Szilard had, as it happened, just realised how such a reaction might theoretically be achieved, and by 1933 was within sight of a patentable procedure. He was, naturally enough, struck by Wells's prescience, and struck too by the fact that the war in the novel had come about because the fictional scientist published his results openly in the traditional scientific way. Bearing in mind what was going on in Germany just then, Szilard did not do this. 'Knowing what this would mean,' he wrote later, ' – and I knew it because I had read H. G. Wells – I did not want this patent to become public. So I assigned it to the British Admiralty.'[1]

Szilard managed to get out of Germany before it was too late and came first to Britain, where a lot of the basic problems of constructing an atomic bomb were being tackled by a varied international team of scientists in the project code-named Tube Alloys. But the work was difficult, and the beginning of wartime shortages meant that only limited resources were available for it, so that progress was slow.

The fear, when the Allies started thinking about the atom bomb, was that the Germans would make one first. The fear was a very realistic one. The universities of Göttingen and Berlin had been among the leading centres of the new physics; and although many of the scientists who had worked there had now fled, many others remained, including Otto Hahn.

No one was more consumed by this fear than Szilard. Distressed by the slow progress of the project in Britain he left for America, determined to bring his ideas, if he could, to the attention of President Roosevelt. After several failed attempts to do this he hit upon the notion of getting Albert Einstein, the most famous scientist in the world, then living at Princeton, New Jersey, to sign a letter introducing Szilard and his recommendations to the President. It was Szilard's belief that once Roosevelt realised how real was the danger that Hitler might get the atom bomb first, he would not hesitate to commit the United States to its own atom bomb project.

In fact this was far from being the immediate effect. The project seemed too far-fetched. The first Einstein letter was received by the President in October 1939. It was not until Einstein wrote to him again in June 1940, pointing out the 'intensification of German interest in uranium since the beginning of the war'[2], information closely followed by a report on the real progress being made by Tube Alloys, that Roosevelt and official Washington became really interested in the atom bomb. The decision to commit resources to it was taken on 6 December 1941 – the day before Pearl Harbor. By the summer of 1942 it was agreed that British and American work in this field should be concentrated in the United States and Canada, and in August 1942, it received the code-name 'The Manhattan Project'. Its main laboratories were established at Los Alamos, New Mexico, under the direction of J. Robert Oppenheimer.

A typical recruit to the project was Joseph Rotblat, a young Polish scientist. When the news of the discovery of fission first reached him, he was working in the Radiological Laboratory in Warsaw. 'By the end of 1938 I had begun to experiment with uranium, so when I heard of the fission of uranium, it did not take me long to set up an experiment to see whether neutrons are emitted at fission. I soon found that they are – indeed, that more neutrons are emitted than produce fission. From my discovery it was a fairly simple intellectual exercise to envisage a divergent chain reaction with a vast release of energy. The logical sequel was that if this energy were released in a very short time it would result in an explosion of unprecedented power.'[3] Clearly other scientists in different countries must also be thinking along these lines.

It did not at first cross Rotblat's mind that he would actually do anything about this idea. For one thing he was a 'pure' scientist, and for another, the notion of working on weapons was abhorrent to him. Anyway, his mind was on other things – he was due to leave Poland to spend a year in England with Professor James Chadwick at Liverpool. At the back of his mind, however, was a worry that would not be put aside. 'In my gnawing fear, the "someone" who might put it into practice was precisely defined: German scientists. I had no doubt that the Nazis would not hesitate to use any device, however inhumane, if it gave their doctrine world domination. . . Throughout the spring and summer the gnawing went on relentlessly. It intensified with the increasing signs that Germany was getting ready for war. And it became acute when I read an article by S. Flugge in *Naturwissenschaft* mentioning the possibility of nuclear explosives.

'Gradually I worked out a rationale for doing research on the feasibility of the bomb. . .'[4]

Inevitably, therefore, Rotblat eventually found himself at Los Alamos, and there, in March 1944, he had a nasty shock. He was staying with the Chadwicks at that time. Chadwick got on well with General Leslie Groves, who was in charge of the Project, and who often came round for a relaxed dinner and a chat. During one of these evenings, it became clear to Rotblat that for Groves the purpose of the bomb was not for use against the Germans at all – or that this was purely incidental. His intended targets were and always had been the Russians – then themselves dying in their millions in order, precisely, to defeat the Germans.

Groves himself never made any bones about this. Testifying in the Oppenheimer hearings in 1954 he said, 'I think it is well known that there was never from about two weeks from the time I took charge of this project any illusion on my part but that Russia was our enemy and that the project was conducted on that basis. I didn't go along with the attitude of the country as a whole that Russia was a gallant ally.'[5]

Ironically, there was never much danger of a German bomb coming to fruition, though of course no one could know this. This was partly because at the start of the war there seemed no need for one, and later there were no resources for such a project; partly because of the effect on German physics of the mass removal of Jewish scientists, and the Jewish taint which hung over the theory of relativity. So far was Germany from producing a bomb of her own that when news of the Hiroshima explosion reached the German atomic scientists then interned in Godmanchester near Cambridge, they were at first quite unable to believe that this was really the work of an atomic bomb. When the news sank in, they were appalled. Otto Hahn said that he felt personally responsible for the deaths of hundreds of thousands of people, since it was his original discovery that had made the bomb possible. He had contemplated suicide when he first saw the full potentialities of his discovery, and now that these had been realised, he felt that he personally was to blame.[6]

When it became clear that the war in Europe would be over before the bomb project was completed, and also that Germany had abandoned her own bomb project, Rotblat knew what to do. 'The whole purpose of my being in Los Alamos had ceased to be, and I asked for permission to leave and return to Britain.'[7] He was the only one of the scientists working at Los Alamos to leave the Project.

It is not easy to take the long view in wartime. Those who do so are not welcomed. Every obstacle was put in Rotblat's way when he left Los Alamos – he knew too much, and the authorities would have liked nothing better than to be able to arrest him on some charge and lock him safely away for the duration. They went to some lengths to prove he was a spy, on his way via Britain to the Soviet Union, but were eventually forced, with great reluctance, to let him go. On the train from Washington to New York, the box containing Rotblat's papers and research notes mysteriously disappeared: he has never seen it since.

Although no one else actually left the Project, Rotblat was not alone in feeling that the Russians should not be treated as enemies in respect of this work. Niels Bohr, who had been dramatically smuggled out of Denmark ahead of the advancing Nazis, was immediately quite clear in his mind as to the dangers of this attitude, and, being enormously renowned and widely revered, was much better placed to get something done about it. In May 1944, he secured a meeting with Churchill in which he tried to persuade him that the Russians must be told what was going on and brought into a scheme to internationalise nuclear energy after the war. But nothing could have been less calculated to appeal to Churchill, then at his most belligerent, than such a scheme; besides which, Bohr was a famously bad advocate. He had a thick accent and a soft voice, and the more important the subject, the more softly he spoke. The interview was a complete failure. All it achieved was that Churchill became very suspicious of Bohr. Roosevelt listened more sympathetically to what he had to say, and promised to raise the matter with Churchill. The result of his doing so was an agreement between Roosevelt and Churchill, in September 1944, that 'The suggestion that the world should be informed regarding [the atomic bomb], with a view to an international agreement regarding its control and use, is not accepted. The matter should continue to be regarded as of the utmost secrecy.'[8] Roosevelt and Churchill jointly initialled an *aide-mémoire* which ended, 'Enquiries should be made regarding the activities of Professor Bohr and steps taken to ensure that he is responsible for no leakage of information to the Russians.'[9]

Rudolf Peierls, who was also seconded from Britain to Los Alamos, was one of the many who did not leave. He wrote: 'I have been asked many times why I continued working for the project when the bomb was no longer needed as a deterrent, and whether I felt happy about developing a weapon that was going to be used to cause unprecedented destruction and suffering. My answer to this question may differ from that of other scientists, but I believe it is not untypical. The war in the Pacific was still raging, with many people being killed and wounded. The possession of the atom bomb would obviously strengthen the Allies' position enormously. Its use on cities was likely to kill and hurt large numbers of civilians, as Frisch and I had pointed out in the very beginning. At that time we felt that a British government would be willing to use such a weapon only in special circumstances, and I felt that the US military and political leaders likewise would not resort lightly to its use. . . The thought that the bomb would be used on a city without warning never occurred to me.'[10]

Peierls was very far from sharing General Groves's view of the real aim of the project. He wrote: 'In thinking about the future, I had no idea of the tension between East and West which would develop and be a major factor in the atomic-weapons problem. I had no illusions about the nature of the Soviet regime but expected that, as we had managed to fight as allies in the war, we would also manage to coexist in peace.'[11]

Meanwhile the pressure was on the scientists to produce results as fast as they possibly could. It was General Groves's abiding fear that the war would end before the bomb could be used.

This opacity as to motive and intent extended from the bomb's construction right through to the decision to use it.

The justification for bombing Hiroshima and Nagasaki has always been that it shortened the war, and so saved hundreds of thousands of lives. Not that, in the weeks immediately following the bombing, the decision needed much justification. A *Fortune* magazine survey published in December 1945 showed that less than 5% of Americans disapproved of the use of the atom bomb on principle, and 22% wished that more such bombs had been dropped quickly, before Japan had a chance to surrender. Even those later to be most active in campaigning against the bomb were, in the post-Hiroshima euphoria, moved to look for a silver lining to the mushroom cloud. J. D. Bernal, writing in the *New Statesman* a week after Nagasaki, was optimistic.

He saw applications for the new source of power in engineering, transport, electrical energy and the provision of food for the starving millions, and pointed out that, so far, the great advances in science had generally been made in the cause of destruction. As for the organisation which had got the project from the lab into production within three years – it was an example of what real cooperation in science could do: the parallel Bernal drew was with the development of penicillin.

But it was not long before worries about the real effects of the bomb began to surface despite the authorities' best efforts to keep them secret. At the same time, the myth of the 500,000 lives saved gained added importance. In February 1947 Henry Stimson, Roosevelt and Truman's Secretary of Defense, wrote in *Harper's*: 'We estimated that if we should be forced to carry this plan (to invade first Kyushu and then Japan's main island of Honshu) to its conclusion, the major fighting would not end until the latter part of 1946, at the earliest. I was informed that such operations might be expected to cost over a million casualties, to American forces alone. Additional large losses might be expected among our allies, and of course, if our campaign was successful and if we could judge by previous experience, enemy casualties would be much larger than our own.'[12]

Winston Churchill, writing six years later, strengthens the myth still further: 'I had in my mind the spectacle of Okinawa island, where many thousands of Japanese, rather than surrender, had drawn up in line and destroyed themselves by hand-grenades after their leaders had solemnly performed the rite of hara-kiri. To quell the Japanese resistance . . . might well require the loss of a million American lives and half that number of British. . . Now all this nightmare picture had vanished. In its place was the vision – fair and bright indeed it seemed – of the end of the whole war in one or two violent shocks. . . To avert a vast, indefinite butchery, to bring the war to an end, to give peace to the world, to lay healing hands upon its tortured peoples by a manifestation of overwhelming power at the cost of a few explosions seemed, after all our toils and perils, a miracle of deliverance.'[13]

This is strong stuff, but there is nothing in the facts of the situation to support it. It has been known for many years – and was certainly known to both these writers – that before the bombs were dropped Japan was a defeated nation, her defences almost non-existent, and that she was actively suing for peace. Alperovitz, in his study of the

8

events leading up to the decision to drop the bomb, showed that, although it was assumed in the spring of 1945, when Truman became President, that the bomb would be used against Japan, it became obvious by the end of June that Japan was defeated. From then on, Truman and his Secretary of State Byrnes, and also Henry Stimson, were more concerned with the bomb's effect on the future position of the Soviet Union. To this end Truman delayed the Potsdam Conference until (he hoped) the first test of the bomb in the New Mexico desert would have taken place; and to this end the bombs were rushed into use the moment they were ready, so that not only would the war be ended quickly, but – crucially – before the Soviet Union entered the Far Eastern theatre by declaring war on Japan. Truman's diary of that period, recently discovered, shows that he knew perfectly well what would happen then. On 17 July, at Potsdam, Stalin told Truman that the Red Army would march into Manchuria; and that day Truman noted in his diary: 'Fini Japs when that comes about.'[14] But Truman and Byrnes deeply did not want Russia to extend its influence over Manchuria and northern China: and what but the bomb was there to stop them?

Where, then, did the mysterious figure of 500,000 American deaths originate? One observer concludes that this must have been an 'off-the-top-of-the-head' estimate made by Stimson in the early spring of 1945 before the Japanese situation deteriorated. Another possibility lies in a letter written by Truman eight days before he left office in answer to an historian's inquiry. Truman wrote: 'I asked General Marshall [at Potsdam] what it would cost in lives to land on the Tokyo plain and other places in Japan. It was his opinion that such an invasion would cost at a minimum a quarter of a million American casualties, and might cost as many as a million, with an equal number of the enemy. The other military men agreed.'[15] But this was an answer to a specific question; whether such an invasion would ever have taken place, given the number of likely casualties and the probability that the war could be ended without it, is of course another matter.

2

Amateurs and Professionals

By the time the first atom bomb was dropped it had already been clear for some time, to those with the information and detachment to sit back and think about such things, that the world after the war would be faced with a crucial choice. Either there would be a nuclear arms race, or this might be avoided by the establishment of some kind of international control over atomic energy. These alternatives were clearly set out by the report of a committee set up under the chairmanship of the distinguished German-born Nobel laureate James Franck, at the Chicago Metallurgical Laboratory, one of the Manhattan Project laboratories. The report was dated 11 June 1945. Part of the preamble to this stated: 'We believe that our acquaintance with the scientific elements of the situation and prolonged pre-occupation with its worldwide political implications, imposes on us the obligation to offer . . . some suggestions as to the possible solution of these grave problems.

'Scientists have often before been accused of providing new weapons for the mutual destruction of nations, instead of improving their well-being. . . However, in the past, scientists could disclaim direct responsibility for the use to which mankind had put their disinterested discoveries. We feel compelled to take a more active stand now because the success which we have achieved in the development of nuclear power is fraught with infinitely greater dangers than were the inventions of the past. . .

'In the past, science has often been able to provide also new methods

10

of protection against new weapons of aggression it made possible, but it cannot promise such efficient protection against the destructive use of nuclear power. This protection can come only from the political organization of the world. Among all arguments calling for an efficient international organization for peace, the existence of nuclear weapons is the most compelling one. In the absence of an international authority which would make all resort to force in international conflicts impossible, nations could still be diverted from a path which must lead to total mutual destruction, by a specific international agreement barring a nuclear armaments race.'[1]

The choice was clear. It was between military secrecy, with its assumption that the United States would, by maintaining the pace of its research, preserve its nuclear lead over the Soviet Union even after the Soviet Union (as was inevitable sooner or later) developed a bomb of her own; and traditional scientific openness, coupled with international control of the new power.

By 4 October 1945, it seemed clear which course the US Government had decided upon. On that day a War Department Bill to establish an atomic energy commission was published. The commission would be part-time and unpaid, except for a full-time administrator and deputy administrator; members of the armed forces might fill these posts or serve on the commission. It could bar at source any information it wished to keep secret, and impose huge fines and long prison sentences (up to $100,000, ten years in jail, or both, for security violations; $300,000 and thirty years for wilful transmission of information).

It was clear that this legislation (the May-Johnson Bill) was being pushed through at top speed, and that as far as the military were concerned, things were still on a war footing, and they intended to keep them that way. An observer commented at this time, 'We are drifting towards a war between the United States and Russia and we are moving towards this war with increasing speed. When the imminence of such a catastrophe first becomes apparent it is usually declared to be "unthinkable", just as the last war was declared to be "unthinkable" around 1934. The threatening conflict has passed beyond that stage and everyone is thinking about it.'[2]

Just how detailed was this thinking on the part of the military was clear from an article by General H.H. (Hap) Arnold published in 1946. He assumed both that Russia would soon get a bomb of her own, and that it would be used. After conceding that the best protection from atomic weapons 'lies in developing controls and safeguards that are strong enough to prevent their use on all sides', he went on to outline what he plainly considered to be a far likelier course of events. 'In the past no effective weapon of war has remained long unused, and in fact the atomic bomb has already brought destruction on Japan.' The general therefore advised that 'no potential aggressor outdistances us in his defense potential', since the side which could expect to survive an atomic exchange would be the first to strike. He considered that the most important passive defence strategy would be the dispersal or burying below ground of essential war industry. 'In a world in which atomic weapons are available, the most threatening program that a nation could undertake would be one of general dispersal and fortification. Should such activities start, the world would see the greatest digging race of all time – and the greatest war.'[3]

Given these expectations, it seemed natural to the military – and especially to General Groves – that the convenient policy of military control and secrecy which had surrounded atomic research for the past five years, should be continued. This might have worried the public, had the public been in any position to know what was happening. But of course it was not. The public was almost entirely unaware of what was going on: and without an informed public there can be no real debate. This was a state of affairs much to the taste of the military – and indeed of governments generally, as was frequently to be demonstrated in the continuing history of nuclear weapons.

There was, however, one group of people both well informed and deeply concerned about what was going on: the scientists whose efforts had actually got the bomb built.

Scientific work is based on the free exchange of information, and on an international scale. As Oppenheimer put it, 'The gossip of scientists who get together is the lifeblood of physics, as I think it must be in all other branches of science.'[4] It had been only with the greatest reluctance and difficulty that the Manhattan Project scientists had allowed themselves to be squeezed into the strait-jacket of military security during the war, and now that it was over, they were impatient for things to get back to normal. Samuel K. Allison, associate director of Los Alamos and the newly appointed director of Chicago's Institute for Nuclear Studies, made this point at a lunch to announce the Institute's formation on 1 September 1945, less than three weeks after

Nagasaki. 'We are determined to return to free research, as before the war,' he said, and warned that, if the exchange of scientific information was prohibited by military regulation, research workers in America would leave the field of atomic energy and devote themselves to study the colours of butterfly wings.[5] (This was known as 'Sam's butterfly speech'.)

The scientists in the various Manhattan Project laboratories now began to form themselves into defined groups – the Association of Los Alamos Scientists, the Association of Oak Ridge Scientists, the Association of Chicago Scientists – later to be subsumed in the all-embracing Federation of Atomic Scientists (FAS). These organisations claimed 95% support from the atomic scientists. Individually and in these joint capacities, they began to agitate against what they saw as the objectionable aspects of the May-Johnson Bill.

The most common criticism of their action took, as might be expected, a form of the 'amateur-professional' line. The scientists, ran this line, had of course every right to protest about the effect of excessive secrecy upon their own work. But when it came to the purely political arena, then their words carried, or should carry, no more weight than those of any other concerned citizen. The kind of indignation their efforts aroused in the military is epitomized by this passage from General Groves's book, *Now It Can Be Told*: 'Unfortunately, the scientific leaders of the project who normally would have been the spokesmen for their colleagues were preoccupied then with getting back to their peacetime occupations at their own universities and I have always felt that they simply did not realize what was developing. The result was that a new and vociferous group of spokesmen arose from among the younger scientific people, few of whom had any experience outside the academic world, and who even there had served in only very subordinate capacities. There were a few others, of course, some of whom sought personal prestige and some of whom wished to forward extreme social points of view. The propaganda emanating from these sources was eagerly seized upon by various ambitious political figures, and by a few people in the State Department who seemed to me more concerned about the momentary good will of other nations than about the welfare of the United States.'[6]

It is not surprising that the military should have objected to the scientists' movement, and on grounds broader than those of the specific issues involved. For one of the things the scientists were trying to do, in their capacity as virtually the only civilians around who were well informed about the potential consequences of nuclear research, was to change the terms of the argument. The military, in rushing the May-Johnson Bill through under the auspices of the War Department, had simply imposed their own world-view virtually unchallenged. And as both sides knew, and still know, nothing affects the course or outcome of any argument more than the terms within which it is conducted.

This fight for the context of the argument has been the fundamental one conducted by the peace movement in its various incarnations since Hiroshima, and it was appropriate, for a variety of reasons, that it should have begun in the United States. It was not just that the United States was the only country to possess and have used atomic weapons. Some fundamental political issues were also at stake.

It is easy to forget in the context of modern politics how recent is the emergence of the United States as a military power. If we take the notion of civilian control as fundamental to the notion of a civilised state (and the very word confirms this identity), then until 1945, and naturally excluding periods when it was actually at war, the United States could be seen as the most civilised of countries. It had never had a standing army – given its secure geographical situation, it had never needed one. It had had its military excursions (as in 1898) but they were excursions, not part of a colonialist way of life. The country had been founded, and its constitution written, by people who had themselves recently thrown off the shackles of colonialism. The State to which they aspired was very different to the European models with which they were familiar.

Partly as a result of all this, the United States had (and has) a political system specifically designed to give the public access to the lawmakers, and one which allows them to make their views effectively felt on specific points of policy. It was this system that the scientists now began to put into action.

Up to a point, of course, the scientists were the arbiters of the fate of atomic energy (as it was then always called) in a way that no one else was. Without their frenzied efforts, the whole thing would still be in the realm of theory; and without their continued cooperation, there would be no scientific progress in this direction. Norbert Wiener pointed along this possible road in an article in the *Atlantic Monthly,*

14

where he described how he had refused someone who wrote to him for a copy of a paper he had written during the war on controlled missiles, and which was now both declassified and out of print. 'The experience of the scientists who have worked on the atomic bomb has indicated that in any investigation of this kind the scientist ends by putting unlimited powers in the hands of the people whom he is least inclined to trust with their use,' he wrote. '. . . If therefore I do not desire to participate in the bombing or poisoning of defenseless peoples – and I most certainly do not – I must take a serious responsibility as to those to whom I disclose my scientific ideas.'[7] This kind of action still remains an option, as the large number of scientists who refuse to work on SDI have shown. However, as SDI also shows, unless this action is more or less unanimous, it cannot be effective – and intellectual excitement, career prospects and differing views on patriotism will ensure that it never is unanimous.

As an informed pressure group, however, the Federation of Atomic Scientists might have some effect. The FAS was launched into action from a fourth-floor apartment in Washington at the beginning of November 1945. Most of the activists were young men, since they were the ones who had the energy and could find the time – though distinguished elders, particularly Harold Urey and Leo Szilard, gave help and support.

What chiefly alarmed the scientists, apart from the May-Johnson Bill's proposal that military control be continued, was the attitude among both legislature and public to secrecy. Henry Stimson, who now deeply regretted the consequences for US/Soviet relations of dropping the bombs, as his last act before retirement presented the President (on 11 September 1945) and the Cabinet (on 12 September) with a memorandum detailing the desirability of international control. With the exception of Henry Wallace, the Secretary of Commerce, who proposed that atomic secrets be shared at once as a gesture of international confidence, the other cabinet members displayed a remarkable lack of enthusiasm for Stimson's proposals, ranging from guarded agreement on the part of Dean Acheson to complete rejection from other members. It was Wallace who made the headlines, and a newspaper poll showed how profoundly out of step both he and the scientists were with public opinion (and therefore with opinion's faithful reflector, Congress). Ninety per cent of those questioned were against giving up the secrets of the bomb.[8]

Undeterred, and armed with their three-line slogan: *There is no secret; There's no defense; International control* – the scientists set about lobbying the lawmakers.

Aims and tactics for lobbying on Capitol Hill are clearly defined. The aim is to get the ear, and if possible the support, of as many Senators and Congressmen as possible for the lobbyist's particular cause. This can be done directly, through meetings and other direct approaches, and indirectly, through general publicity and the application of public pressure from home States and districts. This, in its turn, requires organisation and funds.

When it came to making initial contacts, the scientists were in a good position. They were the men of the moment. It was through their efforts (or so everyone believed) that the war had been brought suddenly to an end. As one recalled, 'I remember in my stint in Washington, I would go to the office of a congressman or a senator, knock on the door, and the door would open and I would walk in and say, "I'm Bernard Feld, I've just come from Los Alamos" – and the red carpet would be spread out. We were great heroes then.'[9]

The story of the scientists' fight has been told elsewhere in great detail. They visited senators and congressmen in their homes and offices, they attended political parties, they held meetings, they briefed interested newsmen. They liaised with citizens' committees on atomic information and helped coordinate meetings of concerned citizens up and down the country. A considerable fund-raising effort had to be undertaken. For the young men, it was an intensive and exciting political education. There were setbacks such as the Canadian spy scare, when the confessions of a Russian defector, which eventually led to the arrest for treachery of Alan Nunn May, a British atomic scientist, induced a sudden access of paranoia, a presage of the McCarthy years, when all scientists were under suspicion of being spies. Nevertheless they won their way, or appeared to do so. The May-Johnson Bill was defeated, and a new Bill, sponsored by Senator Brien McMahon, specified that the domestic control of atomic power was to be given to a full-time civilian Atomic Energy Commission. Its first Chairman was David Lilienthal, a Roosevelt New Dealer whose organisational and political skills were demonstrated in the brilliant success he had made of the Tennessee Valley Authority.

But although their immediate short-term aim had been realised (albeit that they did not manage to prevent Senator Vandenberg inserting an amendment establishing a Military Liaison Committee to the Commission, which was to be a perpetual thorn in Lilienthal's side), they still had to attain their broader aim: to educate politicians and public about the truly revolutionary nature of the new power, of how it made irrelevant all previous notions of war and secrecy and – stemming from this – of the need to establish an international authority to control it.

The possibility of international control did indeed seem almost real in the early summer of 1946. The first meeting of the new United Nations was about to take place, and Lilienthal and Dean Acheson, Secretary of State, produced a report on how such control might be achieved as a basis for negotiation in the new forum. This report was received with enthusiasm by the public and, apparently, by President Truman. But Lilienthal's heart sank when Truman appointed Bernard Baruch, an elderly and conceited financier, to present America's case in the United Nations. Baruch was not wholly sympathetic to the spirit of the report, and Lilienthal was afraid he might try to water it down on his own account, imposing conditions which the Russians would be sure to find unacceptable. In the event the discussions foundered on points of detail rather than of substance, though whether they ever stood any chance of success after the June and July bomb tests at Bikini may be doubted.

There were many sighs of relief when it became clear that the talks had finally failed. After that, people knew where they stood. The Cold War had begun, and a cloak of secrecy descended once more over the field of nuclear weapons.

And what of the attempt to educate public and politicians about the nature of nuclear war? Even those who were implacably opposed to the bomb and might have been expected to approve were often critical of the scientists' efforts in this direction. The question was – at what point did description of the terrors of the atom become counter-productive? After a certain point, people cannot be persuaded to listen to what they do not want to hear. Or they may become apathetic, or terrified into belligerence. 'The news of the dropping of the atomic bomb produced, particularly among the American and to a certain extent among the British people, a great feeling of fear,' wrote J.D. Bernal in 1949. 'The fear, which was natural enough, was exaggerated with the best intentions by naive scientists who wished to scare the world into abandoning the weapon. It was in fact skilfully used to

17

produce the opposite effect of justifying the most lavish expenditure of public money on the production of even more horrible weapons as the only means of defence through retaliation.' Bernal quoted Churchill's Llandudno speech in this connection: 'Nothing stands between us today and complete subjugation to Communist tyranny but the atom bomb in American possession.'[10] This quandary – how much to tell – remains unsolved: a delicate balance, not of terror but of information.

Not that all that much seemed to have sunk in about the special nature of atomic weapons, even among those who might have been expected to know about these things. David Lilienthal recounts an occasion in 1948, when the question of civilian control of the AEC was once more being attacked. The Chiefs of Staff, the Secretary for the Navy (Forrestal) and the Secretary of the Air Force (Symington) all wanted the existing arrangements changed. They thought atomic weapons ought to be available for normal testing and practice, just like any others. As Symington put it, ' "Our fellas at Sandia think they ought to have the bomb. They feel they might get them when they need them and they might not work. . . It is just like having some goods you manufactured, well, when the salesmen go out on the road with it, they learn about the troubles the customer is griping about, and that way you make it better. . . I talked to some scientists at Los Alamos, and one fellow, I forgot his name, he said he didn't believe the law permitted the military to have the bomb, and I don't believe he thought we ought to use it anyway". . . Royall [one of the Chiefs of Staff], who was sitting there looking glummer and glummer, broke in: "We have been spending 98 per cent of all the money for atomic energy for weapons. Now if we aren't going to use them, that doesn't make any sense." '[11]

So much for education. But the FAS was not discouraged. Every month it continued to produce its publication, the *Bulletin of the Atomic Scientists* – still the most interesting and well-informed voice of those who wish for an end to the arms race. Faith in education is not to be dispelled by mere events.

A moment comes and goes. Some thought the opportunity for international control had gone for ever when the bomb test series at Bikini in the summer of 1946 coincided with Baruch and Gromyko's first session at the United Nations. Some thought it was already past by then – a possibility lost when the decision was taken to use the bomb on a city rather than make a demonstration drop which would show the Russians and the Japanese the capabilities of the new weapons, a course which several had urged. One person who thought this was General Eisenhower. He was in Moscow in late 1945, and observed that 'before the atom bomb was used, I would have said yes, I was sure we could keep peace with Russia. Now I don't know. . . People are frightened and disturbed all over. Everyone feels insecure again.'[12] Irving Langmuir, who attended an international scientific conference in Moscow a month after the war in Europe ended, agreed with this. 'In all the speeches,' he reported, 'great emphasis was laid on the international character of science. It was stated that scientists the world over had always cooperated with one another, antagonisms playing no role. Hope was expressed that in other fields nations might learn to co-operate in a similar way. The use of the atomic bomb in August against Japan must have come as a great shock. Most of the Russians probably felt that the security they thought they had reached was suddenly ended. . . I believe that the difficulty of reaching international agreement with Russia before the Moscow conference was caused by a national reaction arising from their disappointment regarding future security.'[13] The then British and American ambassadors to the Soviet Union both endorsed this view.[14]

Of course Russia knew about the possibility of an atomic bomb before Hiroshima. Soviet physicists had been part of that pre-war scientific community which had prepared the ground for it, and had had their own 'Uranium Commission' in charge of research since 1940. They also knew that the Americans and British were working on such a weapon, partly because of the activities of Klaus Fuchs, who was passing on Manhattan Project material, partly because a young Soviet physicist, studying the scientific journals to see if there had been any reaction to the discovery of spontaneous fission, in which he had participated, was struck instead by the glaring absence of any such discussion, concluding that this pointed to the existence of a secret research project in this area. But until the Potsdam conference, when Truman made his throwaway remark about the Americans having 'a new weapon of unusual destructive force', the Soviet project had been confined to a relatively small scale, there being clearly no hope of any Russian atom bomb being ready before the end of the war. Stalin's reaction to Truman's remark and to the subsequent use of the bomb was what might have been expected. He summoned the People's

Commissar of Munitions, his deputies, and Igor Kurchatov, the leading Russian nuclear physicist, to the Kremlin. 'A single demand of you, comrades,' he said. 'Provide us with atomic weapons in the shortest possible time. You know that Hiroshima has shaken the whole world. The equilibrium has been destroyed. Provide the bomb – it will remove a great danger to us.' He then asked how long it would take to build an atomic bomb if they received all the support they needed. Kurchatov estimated five years.[15]

Certainly the window of opportunity for international control was not open long. By 1947, the cold war was well under way. Then, in 1949, an event occurred which changed everything. It was recorded by David Lilienthal, one of the first to hear of it:

'11 p.m. Monday night, Sept 19. Driving up to "Norton Circle" returning . . . from dinner . . . in Edgartown. A heavy ground-fog. Just at the Circle (the Wuthering Heights background of the goat field and its boulders faintly visible), the headlights pick out the figure of a man, hatless, squinting into the lights, looking bemused, hooking his thumb in the hitchhiker's gesture (though, of course, there's nothing to hitch to but the gate). I said quietly, "It's Jim McCormack" (being Brigadier-General James McCormack, AUS, Director of the Division of Military Applications of the US Atomic Energy Commission). As if I frequently found him on a windswept moor, in the dead of night, on an island, outside a goat field. It was he. No questions; said he had lighted a candle in our house. Had he parachuted; what was this?

'11.30 p.m. . . .General Jim and I lighted a kerosene lamp in this room, with its Charles Addams cartoon flavor, esp. at night. He said things jestingly (in part), about the traditionally rude fate of messengers with bad news. Then he gave me the news, rather deadpan, its unambiguous nature rather fuzzy.'[16]

The news, of course, was that Russia had just exploded her first atomic bomb. Kurchatov had beaten his estimate by a full year.

20

3

Under the Counter

The operations of the Federation of Atomic Scientists were a copybook illustration of how the American political system was designed to respond to public pressure – but also of the limits of that system. A lot of information (though much less than today) was freely available to interested parties, and quite open lobbying went on by interest groups – the FAS, the military – to press their particular interests. The public was drawn directly into the fight. On the other hand, such a campaign, to be effective, must limit itself to specific aims – the more limited, the more chance of success. The FAS won their point: the Atomic Energy Commission was controlled by civilians. But, as subsequent history showed, the benefits they hoped would flow from this victory – most importantly, a grasp of the way the new weapon must transform the whole concept of war – were not achieved.

Nevertheless, the subject had undoubtedly been aired in public, and if the American public's interest soon veered off in other directions, that's what happens in politics. No one could claim that the subject had not been discussed. This was not the case in Britain, where the whole question of whether or not Britain should make its own bomb was settled without reference to the public, Parliament or even the Cabinet. By the time the American sociologist Edward Shils remarked, in February 1947, on the almost total silence of parliament, press and public on the subject ('only the *Manchester Guardian*,' he wrote, 'found this significant event [the Atomic Energy Bill] worthy of a leader'[1]) all the important decisions had been taken and fundings had been made.

The way in which press, public and parliament were kept in total ignorance of what was happening about the development of a British bomb so that decisions could be made in the comfortable privacy favoured by Whitehall has been described by Margaret Gowing.[2] What C. P. Snow dubbed 'the euphoria of secrecy and the euphoria of gadgets' had taken over, and the atmosphere of the British civil service, where so much is done informally, by personal contact between old friends, could not have been more congenial to it. When the Minister of Supply, George Strauss, wanted to rationalise the secret and devious arrangements for atomic research in 1947, and was casting around for ways to do this with the minimum of public fuss and disclosure – for example, by using the semi-voluntary D-notice arrangements whereby the press agreed to keep quiet about certain topics – the Ministry of Defence got very irritated. 'Their main objective was to be able to tell people engaged on research into atomic weapons what they were doing, and this, they thought, could be done without any special public announcement. It was after all common practice in government service for staff to deal with matters of the highest secrecy about which there was no publicity of any kind. The whole atomic energy organisation, said the Ministry of Defence bitterly, "has a curious 'barbed wire' mentality of which this is only one example." '[3] The press, however, would not accept a D-notice without some kind of public announcement, so an unobtrusive Parliamentary Question was tabled on 12 May 1948 in which Mr George Jeger asked the Minister of Defence whether he was satisfied that adequate progress was being made in the development of the most modern types of weapon. The Minister assured him that it was. So the British atomic bomb programme proceeded simply because it was assumed by almost everybody that it would proceed. There was no need for discussion. The McMahon Act, with its veto on the passage of technical information between the US and any foreign power, precluded a cooperative effort. There was no guarantee that America would come to Europe's aid in an emergency, and in any case, to rely on American nuclear defence would mean subordinating Europe to American defence policies (as has indeed happened). It was unthinkable that Europe should have no answer of her own to a nuclear threat – and where but in Britain, where so much of the initial work had been done,

22

and whose scientists had worked at Los Alamos, should that answer be provided?

But assumptions are not necessarily facts, and any suggestion that there might be facts worthy of discussion was discouraged. Even such a minor matter as the provision of photographs of the civilian atomic research facility at Harwell for an educational exhibition train organised by the British Association of Atomic Scientists – a politically quite uncontentious body – was greeted with horror, and as few as possible provided. Lord Cherwell, a vice-president of the Association, when questioned on the comparison between the liberal American attitudes to publicity on this subject by comparison with the paranoia evident in Britain, said that there were factors in America which did not exist in Britain, namely, a large bomb stock; relative immunity from retaliation; and 'national pride and the absence of any political opposition from Pacifists or pseudo-Communists.'[4]

Thus by 1950, in peacetime and amid the stringent shortages of the post-war years, it was estimated that out of a science expenditure just over 14 times greater than that of 1936–7, research on food consumed 4 times its pre-war resources; research on health, 4.4 times more; university research, 2.8 times more; and military research and development, 33.7 times more.[5] Even allowing for the fact that Cold War fever was at its height, this seemed disproportionate. But, possibly because nobody knew, nobody complained.

The French political theorist Alain Touraine has said that a social movement's success depends on the precision with which it identifies its antagonist. The British government, in taking such care that no object of antagonism should become visible, had effectively removed the first condition for protest. A similar point was made by the American C. Wright Mills. He said: 'The immediate cause of World War III is the preparation of it. . . In both Russia and America, the ruling circles are possessed by the military metaphysic. . . The pivotal decision made by the elite is in accordance with this military metaphysic. . . It rests upon the dogmatic view – held, I am sure, with sincerity and good intention – that only by accumulating ever and ever greater military peril can a condition of peace be created. The key moral fact about it is the virtual absence within ourselves of opposition to this definition of world reality, to the elites' strategy and policies. The key political and intellectual result is the absence within

Russia and within America, among publics and masses, of any truly debated alternatives.'[6] If this was true in America, it was doubly true in post-war Britain.

But there were other reasons for the lack of protest, less apparent at this distance. One was that people who were later to be numbered among the bomb's staunchest opponents, finding the voice whose absence Mills lamented, were much more equivocal to begin with. Those scientists who had lived with the project from the start had by now overcome their initial intellectual euphoria and could see the awful possibilities. But others, to whom Hiroshima was the first revelation of what had been achieved, were less clear-sighted. J. B. S. Haldane's first reaction, in the *Daily Worker*, was, 'To sum up, I welcome the atomic bomb.' But by 1955 he was writing, 'I have received several invitations to visit Harwell in recent months, and refused them with some rancour, as I hope that, had I been a German, I should have refused invitations to visit Auschwitz or Belsen in 1942. I take the view that the mass killing of civilians is murder, whether it is done with gas chambers or atomic bombs.'[7]

Certainly the notion of a preventive war, in which Russia would be wiped out before she was in a position to inflict much, if any, reciprocal damage, was widespread at this time. *Collier's Magazine* devoted an entire issue to the subject in October 1951. This special issue was, Collier's claimed, the result of many months spent in 'study and consultation with top political, military and economic thinkers – including high-level Washington officials.' The aim of the study, code-named 'Operation Eggnog' was 'to demonstrate that if The War We Do Not Want is forced upon us, we will win.' This war would not last long, *Collier's* assured its readers, and victory for the United States would be assured when 'Task Force Victory' dropped parachutists into the enemy's underground A-bomb vault in the Urals and destroyed all of Stalin's atom bombs. (I.F. Stone, the radical journalist, commenting on this issue, remarked: 'The Urals cover a lot of territory, about as much as our Rockies. Suppose the parachutists don't find the exact spot? Suppose they are overwhelmed by guards? Suppose not all the Russian atom bombs are in that one place? Suppose they are not in the Urals at all? Or suppose Stalin, on reading the issue of *Collier's* (it is intended as a warning to the Kremlin), at once orders his atom bombs taken out of the Urals and distributed among scattered hiding places in Siberia and the Russian Arctic, even

24

placing a few spares for emergency under Molotov's bed? What, then, happens to the course of the war?'[8])

But others, clearer-minded and less inclined to fantasy, also supported this notion at this time, of whom easily the most retrospectively surprising was Bertrand Russell.

Russell was no stranger to controversial political activity. He had been imprisoned as a conscientious objector during World War I, and during the last twenty years of his life was one of the moving spirits – indeed, the figure-head – of the anti-bomb movement. This led many to assume that he was a dangerous Red. But this was far from the truth. He was implacably anti-Communist, and when the bomb was dropped on Hiroshima, he immediately perceived its implications. In a letter written in September 1946 he said: 'There is no point in agreements not to use the atomic bomb as they would not be kept. Russia is sure to learn soon how to make it. I think Stalin has inherited Hitler's ambition for world dictatorship. One must expect a war between USA and USSR which will begin with the total destruction of London. I think the war will last 30 years, and leave a world without civilised people, from which everything will have to be built afresh – a process taking (say) 500 years. . . There is one thing and one only which could save the world, and that is a thing which I should not dream of advocating. It is, that America should make war on Russia during the next two years, and establish a world empire by means of the atomic bomb. This will not be done.'[9] His bashfulness about advocating this policy in public was short-lived. By January, 1948 he was doing so, adding, 'The argument that I have been developing is as simple and as unescapable as a mathematical demonstration.'[10]

Even after the Russians had developed their own atomic bomb in 1949, Russell was slow to change his views. In an article entitled 'Is a Third World War Inevitable?' published in 1950 he wrote, 'I do not agree with those who object to the manufacture of the hydrogen bomb. All arguments for a unilateral limitation of weapons of war are only logically defensible if carried to the length of absolute pacifism, for a war cannot be worth fighting unless it is worth winning. I think also, for the reasons given above, that every increase of Western strength makes war less likely. I do not think that, in the present temper of the world, an agreement to limit atomic warfare would do anything but harm, because each side would think that the other was evading it.'[11]

It is perhaps not surprising, in view of his later opinions and position, that Russell later tended to gloss over these early reactions to the bomb, or even to deny that he had ever said such things. But once, discussing them in a television interview with John Freeman in 1959, he did enlarge on them somewhat. He said: 'It's entirely true and I don't repent of it. It was not inconsistent with what I think now. What I thought all along was that a nuclear war in which both sides had nuclear weapons would be an utter and absolute disaster. There was a time, just after the last war when the Americans had a monopoly of nuclear weapons and offered to internationalize nuclear weapons by the Baruch proposal, and . . . I did think that great pressure should be put upon Russia to accept the Baruch proposal, and I did think that if they continued to refuse it might be necessary actually to go to war.' (In fact Russell had been advocating preventive war before the Baruch proposal was put.) 'At that time nuclear weapons existed only on one side, and therefore the odds were the Russians would have given way.'

Asked whether, if they had not given way, he would have been prepared to face the consequences of using nuclear weapons on the Russians, Russell replied, 'I should. They were not, of course, nearly as bad as these modern weapons are. They hadn't yet got the hydrogen bomb, they had only the atom bomb (and that's bad enough, but it isn't anything like the hydrogen bomb). I thought then, and hoped, that the Russians would give way, but of course you can't threaten unless you're prepared to have your bluff called.'[12]

But by then, largely due to people supporting the policies Russell had been advocating, a chance to at least limit the arms race to atomic (as opposed to thermo-nuclear) weapons had been missed. After the Russians exploded their bomb, debate in America centred on whether or not the hydrogen bomb – the 'super' feverishly propounded by Edward Teller – should or should not be developed. A majority of those on the Atomic Energy Commission's General Advisory Committee, including J. Robert Oppenheimer, erstwhile head of the Los Alamos Laboratory, advised against the new weapon. The issue was never debated in public, since the matter was naturally top secret. The military, and their friends among politicians and in the weapons laboratories, won the day. 'At that time,' wrote David Lilienthal, 'there might have been an opportunity to try something bold and imaginative entirely outside the weapons field, to improve the prospects of peace, but our obsession with bigger bombs as a cure-all excluded any serious consideration of such a possibility. Who can say today with assurance that such an imaginative move might not have changed the grim course of subsequent history?'[14]

'Democratic processes have been one of the first victims of nuclear fission,' noted the indefatigable I. F. Stone in 1955, observing that 'At first from necessity and later from considerations of military security and finally from fear and habit, atomic decisions have been and are being made in secret, without popular consultation.'[14] President Eisenhower, who in 1945 had been against the use of 'that awful thing' and who had noted while he was in Moscow the effect it had had of undermining Russian confidence, so lessening any chances of co-operation between the two great powers, was now committed to the Cold War. His slogan was, 'Keep the public guessing.'

In Britain, too, the public was kept guessing. When Sir Winston Churchill was returned to power in 1951, he made a great point of announcing that the Conservatives would continue with the programme of atomic research for an independent British deterrent initiated by Labour, thus putting the responsibility firmly on Attlee's shoulders while giving an appearance of openness to his own policies. But this openness was for appearances only. The Labour government had concealed, so far as it could, the existence of the programme; the Conservatives admitted its existence, but took great pains to conceal everything else about it.

On 4 March 1954, a Cabinet committee chaired by Churchill agreed on a scheme to disguise the extent of Britain's atomic programme by using such headings as 'other current expenditure' and 'extra-mural research'. The committee agreed that the expenditure estimates of the new Department of Atomic Energy (which was to become the Atomic Energy Authority) 'should be so presented as to conceal the total receipts in respect of atomic weapons and uranium sales.' The reasons for this secrecy were twofold. One, put by the then Minister of Supply, soon to become the Minister for Defence, Duncan Sandys, was that without secrecy 'it will be evident to all that the rate of build-up of our stockpile of atomic weapons is exceedingly slow and that for several years to come Britain's atomic power is not a factor to be reckoned with.'

The second had to do with public opinion. It was decided in June 1954, that Britain should start producing her own hydrogen bomb.

The Cabinet recognised that this decision would offend the consciences of 'substantial' numbers of people in Britain. But ministers argued that 'insofar as any moral principle was involved, it had already been breached by the decision of the Labour Government to make the atomic bomb.' Churchill told his Cabinet colleagues, in an aside that reveals the real attraction of nuclear weapons for political egos, 'We could not expect to maintain our influence as a world power unless we possessed the most up-to-date nuclear weapons.' Sir Norman Brook, Secretary to the Cabinet, minuted: 'The further point was made that, if we were ready to accept the protection offered by United States use of thermo-nuclear weapons, no greater moral wrong was involved in making them ourselves.' Nevertheless, although ministers' consciences were clear, they did not wish to be bothered with other people's. A committee chaired by Norman Brook discussed demands by India that nuclear states should give more information about the effects of the weapons. A note prepared for this committee said that publicity could damage the West's defence interests, not because the Russians might learn something new, but because of the effect on public opinion. The note went on: 'If information about these effects is to be published, the manner of its presentation will need to be carefully considered, because not only is the man in the street more fearful about comparatively mysterious forces like radioactivity than he is about the immediate effects of bomb damage, but also he will be confused by conflicting scientific opinions.'[15] To avoid this, as few such opinions as possible were to be put before him. In 1955, the Director General of the BBC issued a directive forbidding negotiations for broadcasts about nuclear weapons without prior approval by him of a general outline of both programme and speakers. It was not long before Norman Brook himself became Chairman of the BBC's Board of Governors. In this capacity he was chiefly responsible, in 1964, for ensuring that Peter Watkins's famous film *The War Game* was not shown – a film which would undoubtedly have put the wind up the man in the street.

Not that the man in the street, at this point, seemed to be showing much interest in the subject. In February 1955, the left-wing weekly *New Statesman and Nation* ran a three-and-a-half page supplement on 'The Dilemma of the H-Bomb'. This concluded that Britain must accept the H-bomb as a fact and reshape both her armoury and her policies to take account of it. Richard Crossman, one of the intellectual leaders of the left, and at that time an opposition MP, recorded in his diary that many of his fellow left-wingers 'were . . . appalled by this idea and felt that the Left should choose the manufacture of the H-bomb as their great issue for the next Party Conference.' Next day, he took the theme up again. 'Despite what Barbara (Castle) says, I doubt whether this will in fact, over the long run, be a great issue in the Party or in the country,' he concluded. The *Daily Mirror* had devoted its front pages the previous Friday and Saturday to the subject, and had received a total of ten letters in response. Another Labour MP, Arthur Creech-Jones, agreed with Crossman. He said, 'They're not interested because they always assumed we'd got it already and that, even if we hadn't, we were bound to make it in a world as crazy as this.' 'To run a campaign against an accomplished fact is difficult at the best of times,' was Crossman's opinion.[16]

Nevertheless, despite the best efforts of those in authority, the man in the street was beginning to get some funny ideas.

4

Protest

There had, of course, been anti-bomb protests from the beginning, in Europe as well as America. The World Peace Council, headed by such names as J. D. Bernal and Frederic Joliot-Curie, had been set up in Stockholm in 1950, and had been vociferously denouncing the bomb ever since, but this was easily discounted by those who wanted to discount such things, and distrusted even by those who didn't, because the WPC was generally regarded as a communist front organisation.

Despite the blanket lack of information, however, disquiet was mounting. The focus of protest this time was not the United States. The heady days of the atomic scientists' raid on Washington were long gone. Even to moot such action in the 1950s would mean risking one's livelihood. The Russian bomb and the Fuchs and Nunn May spy trials had all contributed to the mounting wave of anti-communist hysteria and general xenophobia so skilfully exploited by Senator Joe McCarthy. It became dangerous to express even mildly liberal opinions. Robert Oppenheimer, a member of the General Advisory Committee, which had advised against development of the H-bomb, and now head of the Institute of Advanced Studies at Princeton, had his security clearance removed and could no longer be privy to the secrets of the atomic age which he had been instrumental in initiating. Another of the atomic scientists, Dr Edward Condon, who had been at Chicago and was subsequently head of the National Bureau of Standards, was hounded from his job and could find no other until Washington University at St Louis, a stronghold of liberalism, took

30

him in. Countless similar stories could be (and have been) told.

Nevertheless, even in McCarthyite America, the authorities were aware that public complacency was easily shattered. The Atomic Energy Commission was worried when, in 1953, a test code-named 'Simon' contaminated upstate New York, while 'Harry' spread 6 rems of radiation in one day on the town of St George in southern Utah, 200 km. east of the test site at Yucca Flats, Nevada[1] (the current figure for maximum civilian exposure is 0.5 rems a year). 'In the present frame of mind of the public, it would take only a single illogical and unforeseeable incident to preclude holding any further tests in the United States,' the AEC noted.[2] But in the stifling atmosphere of the McCarthy witch-hunts, concerted protest in America was an unlikely eventuality.

The same was not true of Europe, however. There had already been disquiet in Britain – not least among the military – when America was permitted to establish nuclear-capable airbases there at the time of the Berlin crisis in 1948. By the mid-fifties, when Russia had her own H-bomb, there was anxiety that Britain, with both her own bombs and the American bases on one small, densely populated island, would be a sitting target for the rockets recently set up in Central Europe, with their nuclear-tipped warheads. It was admitted that, in the case of nuclear attack, there was no possible adequate protection for the civilian population.[3]

There was a foretaste of things to come in 1952, when a few British pacifists who had spent the previous winter demonstrating outside the War Office decided they wanted to make a more direct protest against the British bomb, preferably at the place where it was made. But where was that? Everyone knew that atomic research went on at Harwell, but that was (as the publicity constantly reiterated) civilian research. There had to be another place. In the words of Hugh Brock, one of the War Office protesters, they 'had no clue to the bomb plant until someone suggested that there was another Atomic Energy Research Establishment in the Reading area which might be the place. It came from one of those types who are gluttons for bus timetables and seem to absorb every detail in them. He had noticed a bus stopping at "the AERE", and it certainly wasn't at Harwell. It was near a little village called Aldermaston.'[4] Brock went down to reconnoitre and found an enormous building programme under way to house a military project of which almost everyone in Britain was ignorant. A coach was hired, and on 19 April, thirty-five people went down to demonstrate at Aldermaston. The next demonstration there occurred in 1958; by that time the designation was no longer AERE (Atomic Energy Research Establishment) but AWRE (Atomic Weapons Research Establishment). The bus enthusiast's hunch had been correct.

But how could anything be done to stop the burgeoning nuclear arms race? The initiative was taken by Bertrand Russell. He felt that, if enough people could be awakened to the gravity of the situation, it might be possible to raise a big enough public outcry to force the politicians to act. In June 1954, he wrote to the BBC: 'In common with everybody else, I am deeply troubled about the prospects for mankind in view of the H-bomb. I have a profound desire to do whatever lies in my power to awake people to the gravity of the issue.'[5] He proposed a broadcast talk, which was eventually transmitted on 23 December, entitled 'Man's Peril'.

The effect of the broadcast — its calm but terrifying content enhanced by the Christmas timing — was extraordinary (and was probably instrumental in leading to the instruction from the Director-General already mentioned that no such thing should ever be commissioned unsupervised again). Russell had asked whether the human race was 'so destitute of wisdom, so incapable of impartial love, so blind even to the simple dictates of self-preservation, that the last proof of its silly cleverness is to be the extermination of all life on our planet.' Floods of letters from all over the world testified to the universality of this desperate worry.

What, however, was to be done next? People were worried — but the worry had to be channelled in order to affect the politicians. Others, as concerned as Russell and as eminent, had been trying to do this for years. One such was Frederic Joliot-Curie, the pioneering French nuclear physicist. He now wrote to Russell.

Joliot was a Communist who had fought in the French Resistance, taken charge of France's post-war nuclear reactor programme and then been sacked for his political views. He was now the President of the World Federation of Scientific Workers, and as such had already tried unsuccessfully to convene an international meeting on the dangers of nuclear weapons. He said in his letter: 'The danger that faces humanity appears so terribly real that I believe it essential for scientists whom people respect for their eminence to come together to prepare an objective statement on the matter.' The Federation had met

32

with some difficulties in trying to get together such a statement, since many people declined to be associated with what they saw as a Communist organisation, however much they personally might agree with it in this respect. 'Such doubts,' wrote Joliot, 'would vanish if some great, universally respected figures, such as yourself, gave the support of their great authority to the idea of a conference.' Russell replied, cautiously agreeing: 'We all have our prejudices in favour of one side or the other, but in view of the common peril it seems to me that men capable of scientific detachment ought to be able to achieve an intellectual neutrality, however little they may be neutral emotionally.' He then wrote to Einstein, asking if he knew any Americans who would help.[6]

The task of drafting the statement was not easy. Eventually a wording was arrived at which was acceptable to both Communists and non-Communists because it refrained from mention of any details likely to offend either. Russell sent a copy of the revised statement off to Einstein. He then flew to Rome to address a conference of the World Association of Parliamentarians for World Government. On his way back to Paris, the pilot added to the flight details the item of news that Albert Einstein had just died in Princeton. 'I felt shattered,' commented Russell, 'not just for the usual reasons but because I saw my plan falling through without his support.'[7] But waiting for him in Paris was a letter from Einstein agreeing to sign the amended statement.

The document agreed to by Einstein stated that the nuclear peril was more important than any ideological split between Communism and the West. All the potential signatories agreed to this in principle, but Einstein's death created a difficulty: the document could not now be altered if it were to retain his signature, and several of the potential signatories – most importantly, Joliot-Curie – would have liked to make further modifications. The problem was eventually overcome by allowing Joliot to publish his reservations as footnotes to the main document. By the end of May 1955, Russell had collected seven signatures: Percy W. Bridgman and Hermann J. Muller from the USA; Cecil F. Powell and Joseph Rotblat from England; Leopold Infeld from Poland; Hideki Yukawa from Japan; Max Born from Germany. Linus Pauling signed soon afterwards. Of these, only Rotblat and Infeld were not Nobel laureates. Born's name was omitted from the announcement of what came to be known as the Einstein-Russell

Manifesto, because he had prefaced his letter of agreement with such a strong anti-communist proviso that Russell had assumed he must be refusing to sign and had not troubled to read the rest of the letter closely enough.

The Manifesto was presented on 9 July 1955 at a meeting chaired by Rotblat. It was essentially a redrafted version of Russell's Christmas broadcast. It set out the appalling consequences of a nuclear war, called for a meeting of scientists from both sides of the Iron Curtain, and proposed that these scientists should then urge all governments to admit that it was no longer possible to further their purposes by war.

The combination of Einstein's dramatic death-bed signature, mounting public disquiet and the starry list of signatures (even though many of the names meant little to the general public) generated an unexpectedly large and enthusiastic coverage. Various groups, and Russell himself, worked as hard as they could to keep the momentum going, but the events of the next year, the 1956 Hungarian uprising and the abortive Suez invasion, diverted public attention.

It was at this low point that a wealthy Canadian industrialist, Cyrus Eaton, stepped in. Eaton had met Russell years before at Chicago University, of which he was a trustee. He had welcomed the Manifesto from the start, and had already tried to persuade Russell to convene the scientists' conference at his home village of Pugwash in Nova Scotia, but it had seemed altogether too remote. Now, however, no such offer, however remote the location, could be turned down. But would the Canadian government allow the Communist scientists in without trouble? Eaton ensured that it would; and in July 1957, the Pugwash Conference took place, attended by twenty-two physicists, biologists and chemists.[8] It became an annual event, and has retained the name of Pugwash even though the venue changes every year.

As the years went by, and suspicions of propaganda dropped away, both the size and the prestige of the conference greatly increased. It has remained an important meeting-ground, and was instrumental in securing both the Partial Test-Ban Treaty and the mutual ban – which has been observed until now by both sides – on chemical and biological weapons. This was a rare example of superpower co-operation. Both sides got together and agreed on the defects of these weapons. Apart from the peculiar, if illogical, repugnance they arouse, they are hard to control in use and may easily be manufactured quickly and quietly by any small country, which may then make itself a nuisance to the rest of the world. So because it suited both sides, everyone was banned from making them.

The events in Suez and Hungary which so nearly blocked the scientists' initiative had other effects on the public mind. People were frightened, and such statements as that of Field-Marshal Montgomery, in November 1956, did little to reassure them. 'We at SHAPE,' he said, '. . . with the full political agreement of the NATO council, are basing our plans upon the fact that if we are attacked we use nuclear weapons in our defence. The proviso is that the politicians have to be asked first. That might be a bit awkward, of course, and personally I would use nuclear weapons first and ask afterwards.'[9]

Other worries were also surfacing. In November 1955, one of the American Atomic Energy Commissioners, Thomas E. Murray, suggested that there should be a world H-bomb demonstration. The proposal was rejected out of hand. 'The Pentagon and State Department have feared public debate lest it interfere with the task of recasting our armed forces, our moral standards and our minds,' commented I. F. Stone. '. . . To hold an H-bomb demonstration in the Pacific, as Mr Murray proposed, with the world press and all other governments represented, would be not merely to frighten Them but to awaken Us out of our lethargy.'[10] A recent Gallup poll showed that 'peace' was perceived by 42% of the American public as the greatest problem confronting their nation – the farm problem, which came next, drew only 8%.

Besides drawing unwelcome attention to this issue, Mr Murray presented the public with other, related worries. The question of strontium 90, which was soon to outrank all other bomb-related issues in the public mind, made its first appearance. Commissioner Murray revealed that thermo-nuclear explosions produced radioactive strontium; that it was a deadly poison whose contamination lasted long after the blasts themselves were over; and that, as it passed up the food chain into the human body, it could create bone cancer. Estimates of how much of this substance could safely be absorbed by the body had 'changed wildly' over the past year, said Mr Murray. A year earlier it was said there was little to fear because the amount would have to increase by a million times before it reached dangerous levels. This had now been reduced to ten thousand times. 'Mr Murray thinks this figure will be lowered,' reported Stone. 'His four fellow-

Commissioners, in rejecting his proposal for an H-bomb demonstration, significantly fail to deny these figures. Their official statement merely says that until further study has been made "it is impossible to be definite about the genetic effects." This is quite different from the statements of a year ago that fear of radioactive fall-out was exaggerated. . .'[11] The AEC did little to calm public worries by measuring strontium fall-out levels in 'sunshine units'. When Congressmen questioned them as to the exact meaning of this terminology, they dropped it.

Meanwhile, ex-President Truman was invited to Britain to receive an Oxford honorary degree. David Lilienthal had found his exhortation to 'let me do the worrying' about the Bomb reassuring: others did not. A leading Oxford philosopher, Miss G. E. M. Anscombe, published a pamphlet opposing the degree. 'I have long been puzzled by the common cant about President Truman's courage in making this decision [to drop the bomb]', she wrote. 'Of course, I know that you can be cowardly without having reason to think you are in danger. But how can you be courageous? Light has come to me lately: the term is an acknowledgement of the truth. Mr Truman was brave because, and only because, what he did was so bad. But I think the judgment unsound. Given the right circumstances (for instance, that no one whose opinion matters will disapprove), a quite mediocre person can do spectacularly wicked things without thereby becoming impressive.'[12]

In many ways, Miss Anscombe and her pamphlet epitomized the new protest movement that was beginning to assemble itself around the H-bomb issue. Its approach was moral, rather than scientific. It was led by, and largely composed of, middle-class intellectuals. And it was British.

5

CND

During the 1950s, many separate small groups in Britain had been expressing their concern at the seemingly unstoppable nuclear weapons programme. They included Cambridge scientists, the Peace Pledge Union, the Hydrogen Bomb National Campaign, and various local Committees for the Abolition of Nuclear Weapons Tests. In February 1957 these merged to form a National Committee.

Public disquiet mounted during 1957. In April, the first British H-bombs were exploded at Christmas Island in the Pacific. In the same month came Duncan Sandys' controversial Defence White Paper in which he announced that Britain's defences were henceforth to be based upon the nuclear deterrent, and also that there was at present no satisfactory way of protecting the civilian population against a nuclear attack. In the summer, thirty Labour MPs formed an H-Bomb Campaign Committee, which in September rallied 4000 people in Trafalgar Square to oppose British manufacture of the bomb. But in October, at the Labour Party Conference, Aneurin Bevan, the hero of the Left and shadow Foreign Secretary, attacked the nuclear disarmers, condemning their approach as an 'emotional spasm' not to be confused with serious policy, and urging Conference not to send British ministers 'naked to the conference table'. This speech caused rage and despair among Bevan's admirers and followers: it 'seemed to many of us' (wrote J. B. Priestley) 'to slam a door in our faces.'[1] Shortly after this, Russia successfully launched Sputnik, the first artificial satellite. This meant she now had the technology to send missiles as far as the United States, whose location on a distant continent no longer offered automatic military inviolability. Nervousness increased around the world.

The opponents of nuclear arms had for many years found their most effective platform in Kingsley Martin's *New Statesman*. It was he who published the cogent and well-informed articles on strategy and politics by Professor P. M. S. Blackett. Blackett and Sir Henry Tizard, both deeply involved in the scientific conduct of World War II, had alone advised Attlee against the development of a British bomb, and had been summarily disregarded. But Blackett, unlike Tizard, did not retire into despairing silence. The *New Statesman* also published the extraordinary correspondence between Bertrand Russell, Nikita Khruschev and John Foster Dulles (Russell's comment to Kingsley Martin was that it was 'awful that the continued existence of the human race should be dependent upon the whims of a pair of nincompoops'.)[2] Then, in November 1957, following Bevan's speech and the Sputnik launch, the *New Statesman* published J. B. Priestley's piece, 'Britain and the Nuclear Bombs'. In it, Priestley wrote: 'We have all known people in whom was sown the fatal seed of self-destruction, people who would sit with us making sensible plans and then go off and quietly bring them to nothing, never really looking for anything but death. Our industrial civilisation, behaving in a similar fashion, may be under the same kind of spell, hell-bent on murdering itself. But it is possible that the spell can be broken. If it can, then it will only be by an immensely decisive gesture, a clear act of will. . . In plain words: now that Britain has told the world she has the H-bomb she should announce as early as possible that she has done with it, that she proposes to reject, in all circumstances, nuclear warfare. This is not pacifism. There is no suggestion here of abandoning the immediate defence of this island. . . No, what should be abandoned is the idea of deterrence-by-threat-of-retaliation. There is no real security in it, no decency in it, no faith, hope, nor charity in it.'[3]

The response to Priestley's article astonished everyone. So much mail poured in that the *New Statesman* was unable to deal with it. Clearly something had to be done to mobilise this support – but what? Priestley got together what he described as 'a sort of arts-science-etc. non-political group to denounce nuclear warfare'.[4] This group, including Blackett, Russell and George Kennan, the former US ambassador in Moscow, met at Martin's flat 'to discuss' (said Martin) 'the possibility of a national organisation which would supersede the National Committee for the Abolition of Nuclear Weapon Tests'.[5] Others, including members of the NCANWT, were thinking along the same lines. At an inaugural press conference for what had now been dubbed the Campaign for Nuclear Disarmament, Canon Collins, a canon of St Paul's Cathedral who was to share the leadership of the new movement with Russell, announced that its aim was 'a sharp, virile and successful campaign to rid Britain of nuclear weapons, if need be by unilateral action'. The astonishment evoked in today's reader by his choice of adjectives, especially in this context, shows how fast times have changed. His hopes were not to be fulfilled.

Central Hall, Westminster was booked for the Campaign's inaugural meeting on 17 February 1958. The place was packed: 5,000 people came and four overflow halls had to be used. Speakers rushed from one hall to the next. It had been decided that a collection should be taken to raise some initial funds for the new organisation. One scientist attended the meeting with a Russian woman who observed the proceedings with interest. The sight of the collection bags going round astounded her. 'In my country,' she commented, 'you would not need to do this. The organisation would be funded by the state.'[6] Substitute 'be allowed' for 'need' and the difference between anti-nuclear movements in East and West is neatly summarised. There are situations where government funding is not only unnecessary, but strictly inimical to the matter in hand.

The first Aldermaston march took place that Easter. 4,000 people took part – small by today's standards, but impressive then. (But the numbers did not compare with those who turned out in Germany that year to protest against NATO's decision that West Germany must be armed with tactical nuclear weapons. A protest rally in Frankfurt on 23 March attracted 20,000 people, and in Hamburg, 120,000 protested.) This was just the beginning. By early 1959, CND had more than 300 local groups, and opinion polls showed that support for banning the British bomb had risen from 25% in April 1958, to 30% in March 1959.[7]

One of the most noticeable aspects of the nuclear weapons debate is how much more is meant than is ever said in so many words. In Britain between 1945 and 1963 (after which public debate of this issue largely ceased until 1979) the question at issue was Britain's continued existence as a Great Power. This was the spoken and unspoken assumption behind the decision that Britain must have a bomb of her own. It was also, in a curiously parallel way, the assumption of many of the new leaders of the Campaign for Nuclear Disarmament. Time and again their speeches were about Britain's continuing leadership of the world – if no longer as a military power, then by setting a moral example. At the inaugural meeting of CND at Central Hall, Alex Comfort put this very plainly. He said, 'We can make Britain offer the world something which is virtually forgotten – moral leadership. Let us make this country stand on the side of human decency and human sanity – alone if necessary. It has done so before. If it does so again I do not think we need to fear the consequences.'[8] Priestley, in his *New Statesman* piece, had sounded precisely the same note. 'Alone, we defied Hitler; and alone we can defy this nuclear madness into which the spirit of Hitler seems to have passed, to poison the world.'[9] The theme was endlessly repeated by unilateralists (as those who advocated Britain's unconditional abandonment of her nuclear weapons were called), as endlessly as the multilateralists (those who insisted that they, like everyone else, wanted nuclear disarmament, but that Britain should not disarm unless other nations were prepared to make a similar gesture) reiterated the 'naked to the conference table' motif. For the one side the bomb's retention, for the other, its renunciation, constituted Britain's only claim to retain her pre-war status as a world power.

Arguments about nuclear disarmament were also going on in America, and they too featured disagreements between 'multi-lateralists' and 'unilateralists'. Their views of the implications of British nuclear disarmament were rather different from those of CND members. Amitai Etzioni, an American multilateralist, argued against the American unilateral stand by comparison with the British. His argument was that the Americans 'base their position on moral grounds' (and were thus hopelessly unrealistic) whereas the British 'rest their case on logic' (i.e. the British bomb was anyway an irrelevance, so they might as well make the gesture and give it up).[10] Barbara Deming, an American unilateralist (i.e. she thought the Americans should make the gesture and give up their bombs) arguing against Etzioni, wrote: 'Your implication . . . is that a natural gulf exists between morality and logic. I will grant you, sadly, that it is not logical for Bertrand Russell to use moral arguments for England's laying down of arms when he fails to recommend it to all countries. This has always seemed to me a great weakness in his stand.'[11] Russell, the ardent anti-communist, was against America's giving up the bomb if Russia did not also do so; he hoped that Britain's gesture might bring the two to such an agreement. Deming saw no reason why this should be so.

This discrepancy between the transatlantic view of what Britain might accomplish and what seemed possible from London was hard for even the most politically sophisticated Britons to swallow. Dean Acheson's famous speech at West Point caused indignation on both sides of the nuclear divide – but for different reasons. Richard Crossman, a nuclear disarmer, commenting on it in *The Times*, wrote: 'I was appalled by the central theme of the West Point speech, a plea that the Western Alliance should be reorganised in order to help the Germans push the Russians out of East Germany and start the liberation of Eastern Europe. I was even more appalled by the fact that almost all Acheson's British critics swallowed this second part of his speech and only objected because he preceded it with a barbed paragraph about ourselves. "Great Britain", he observed, "has lost an empire and not yet found a role: the attempt to play a separate power role is about played out." And he went on: "Great Britain attempting to work alone and to be a broker between the United States and Russia has seemed to conduct policy as weak as its military power." ' Crossman commented: 'The first sentence may be difficult to swallow; but everyone outside this country knows it to be true. The second sentence need not be true, but it has been made true by those leaders in both the main parties . . . who have tried to keep Britain great by means of a foreign policy based on the Anglo-American alliance, and a strategy centred on the British H-bomb.'[12]

When the FAS set out to wrest control of atomic power from the military, its campaign had two great political advantages. One was that its objective was limited and clearly defined. The other was that it was trying to pre-empt a decision, not to reverse one already taken. CND's political task was far harder. Its objective was not, when one came to examine it, especially clear-cut. Did it want merely to abandon British nuclear weapons or would it expel American ones as well? And if so what about NATO, and what about British defence policy? British nuclear weapons were not just a *fait accompli*, they were (as Duncan Sandys had explained) the basis of Britain's defence strategy.

CND therefore had to contend not merely with the inertia which makes it hard to overturn any well-established policy, but with accusations that they were unpatriotic and wanted to leave the country an undefended target for Russian invaders (in fact, precisely the obstacles still facing it today).

When it came to getting their message across to the public, CND had the edge over the FAS. The leadership of the campaign largely consisted of writers, journalists, and the new wave of dramatists and actors associated with the Royal Court Theatre. These were people whose particular skill lay in getting a message across. And undoubtedly educating the public is important. Public education, in facts and of the imagination, has always been one of the chief aims of the anti-nuclear movement. But the message was also, of course, directed at politicians – and here the members of CND, as opposed to their American predecessors, were in a quandary. In America, where the bureaucracy largely changes with each administration and where every politician stands for election on specific issues, as well as the party ticket, the aim is simple. Build up enough support, on both sides of the house, and your measure – whether at city, State or Federal level – will be adopted. In Britain, however, the party system rules supreme. Any measure – unless it is the kind of non-party 'moral' issue, such as abortion reform or the abolition of capital punishment, which may be introduced by a Private Member's Bill – must be adopted by one or another party, and in order for it to be implemented, that party must then gain power and push it through the bureaucracy. In the case of a highly controversial and deeply political measure such as nuclear disarmament, the party must be very committed to it if it is to be implemented in spite of an unwilling bureaucracy. Yet if an issue such as nuclear disarmament is to gain the necessary public support to force unwilling politicians to take it up, it cannot be presented as a mere party political issue.

CND was faced with an additional difficulty. It might be supposed that massive public support for a particular policy, of the sort it was regularly able to demonstrate over the next few years, might dispose democratically elected politicians in that policy's favour. In the United States this might be the case; in Britain, not necessarily so. British politicians do not take advice from the populace. They take it from carefully selected advisers. The public do not form part of this charmed circle. It is easy to claim that the public does not know the facts, especially when these are carefully kept from them. The claim that demonstrating protestors are a rabble, misled and ill-informed though possibly well-meaning, was then and is still the handiest weapon at the disposition of politicians faced by a crowd in disagreement with current policy.

Of the CND of the late 50s and early 60s, Christopher Driver in his book on the movement wrote: 'Many Conservative MPs who might have had some sympathy with the objects of the Campaign, and who certainly shared its misgivings about the Sandys Defence White Papers, balked at the personalities of the leading Campaigners, and were later confirmed in their distaste by the phenomenon which Peter Simple of the *Daily Telegraph* cruelly christened "Rentacrowd": London's instantly available progressive claque, ready at the drop of a leaflet to demonstrate on a whole range of causes. . . In the Parliamentary Labour Party, the Campaign evoked broadly similar feelings of hostility quite early on. . .'[13] Driver argues that CND may even have been politically counter-productive, that 'its existence and activity . . . actually prevented the nation from passing as swiftly as it should have done from the Excalibur to the Damocles phase in its attitude to nuclear weapons.'

Given the way British politics work, he may be right. But the question then arises – what is the man or woman in the street, who does not have access to the privileged corridors of power, to do? Keep quiet and hope that those who do have such access may eventually come to see things his way? What CND did was to show such people that there was a way in which they could express their feelings and gain huge publicity for them.

Meanwhile, although politicians of every hue objected to this attempt by the public to railroad them into policies they didn't, for their own reasons, like, in practice there was no question which party in Britain, if any, would take up the cause of nuclear disarmament. The Conservatives had just implemented a new defence policy built around the British bomb. The hopes of CND, therefore, lay with the Labour Party – the party which had, under Attlee, inaugurated the British bomb. But would Labour take up the issue? The question was to dominate Labour politics from then on.

Only three years earlier, Richard Crossman had dismissed the H-bomb as 'unlikely ever to be a great issue in the Party or the country'. Now he observed in his diary entry for 10 April 1958: 'How much my whole political life seems to gyrate round nuclear weapons! But, then, it probably is the single greatest issue for us and the one on which the Labour Party is inclined to commit itself with an extraordinary combination of irresponsibility and prejudice.'[14]

No contrast could have been greater than the views of the campaign from inside and outside the Labour Party. Seen from the outside, the issue was enormous – much bigger than party politics. The nuclear arms race was gathering speed. In February 1958 Britain signed an agreement with the United States to build four nuclear missile bases in East Anglia. The opinion polls showed that most people in Britain opposed these bases, and 80% expected less than half of Britain's population to survive a nuclear war. In March, there was the NATO decision that West Germany should be armed with tactical nuclear weapons. Meanwhile more nuclear weapons than ever were being tested – more than 100 in 1958, double the 1957 figure, which in turn was double that of 1956.[15] The most popular speeches at the end of the first of CND's Easter marches – this one was from London to Aldermaston, unlike the later ones which started in Aldermaston and finished with a big rally in London – were those which most clearly dissociated the movement from party politics.

The marchers were lucky. They started on Good Friday, which was a beautiful day. Then Saturday poured with rain, which attracted sympathy, and they had television coverage every day, leading to a fine climax on Easter Monday. The campaign was off to a flying start, publicity-wise at least.

The view from inside the Labour Party, however, was not so simple. Michael Foot, an ardent supporter of the Campaign, might urge CND members to vote Labour with the words, 'Only through the election of a Labour Government and the political pressure which we may exert afterwards can we succeed.' But the leader of the Labour Party, Hugh Gaitskell, was bitterly opposed to nuclear disarmament, as were many of Labour's right-wing – his base of support within the party. On the Tuesday following the march, John Strachey, a Gaitskellite and committed nuclear warrior, published a pamphlet with a foreword by Gaitskell ironically entitled *Scrap All the H-Bombs* (Strachey preferred to use tactical nuclear weapons). Crossman commented, 'I have to admit that after reading it I came to the conclusion that, if his main contention had been correct (namely, that the only logical alternative to pacifism is his own policy), then I would be a pacifist. This sharp dichotomy between nuclear warrior and nuclear abolitionist is, of course, what Gaitskell, Bevan and Brown want in order to keep the party steady in its committal to a nuclear strategy.'[16] The climax of this battle (though by no means the end of the war) was Gaitskell's refusal to accept a Labour Party Conference commitment to nuclear disarmament in 1960, and his promise that he would 'fight, fight and fight again' to get this decision reversed.

What had happened, of course, was that the British bomb had become the focus of the perennial battle between the Left and Right of the Labour Party for the 'soul' of the party. Things within the party got very nasty. Judith Hart, a left-wing unilateralist MP, wrote at this time: 'There's such bitterness: I can't visit some of my friends now. Once defence or Scarborough' (the scene of the 'fight, fight and fight again' speech) 'or Gaitskell come up our arguments are nasty. We can't talk to each other any more.' A member of the Young Socialists, always left-wing and unilateralist, asked which political event had given him greatest pleasure in 1962, replied, 'the death of Hugh Gaitskell.'[17]

Under these circumstances, the prospects for a policy of British nuclear disarmament even should a Labour government be returned seemed at best uncertain. And if the Conservatives remained in office, then of course they were nil.

6

On the March

'When Governments break the law, honest men become revolutionaries. We must, I believe, look forward to a period during which we shall only be able effectively to show our respect for international law by violating the civil and perhaps the criminal law of England.' – J. B. S. Haldane[1]

According to Gallup polls taken at the time, support for CND's line peaked in April 1960, when 33% of respondents, asked 'what policy should Britain follow about nuclear weapons?' replied, 'Give up nuclear weapons entirely.' A year later this figure had fallen to 19%, and the Labour Party's autumn 1961 conference reversed the previous year's commitment to unilateralism.[2] Clearly CND's strategy of sweet reason and mass demonstrations was getting nowhere politically. But what were the alternatives?

This was the question which was to be instrumental in tearing CND apart. But it was also the question which was to lead most directly towards the political future – and not just the future of the peace movement. What had become clear was that there was no way in which British politics, at least, could, or would, deal with a question of vital concern to vast numbers of the people – a concern so great and numbers so large that even the apolitical British were prepared to turn out on the streets in their hundreds of thousands to demonstrate about it. But if the question was not – as clearly it was not – going to be dealt

46

with by the existing political structure, what was to be done? Should that structure be undermined or changed, and if so, how?

Questions such as this – or at any rate the perceptions beneath them – were anathema to many of the leaders of CND. People such as Michael Foot and other left-wing MPs had invested their whole lives in the existing system. The same was true, in a different way, of the *New Statesman* group, who were mostly active in the Labour Party. But there was one person of whom this was absolutely not true, and that was Betrand Russell.

Russell was by now approaching his ninetieth year. He had throughout his life held strong political convictions, usually well outside party lines, and had never hesitated at giving these expression and effect outside the law if necessary. This made him a natural focus for that faction of CND which now thought direct action and civil disobedience would be the most effective way of putting their views across. This group called itself the Committee of 100.

By advocating civil disobedience and passive resistance, Russell was merely returning to policies and principles for which he had first become famous – or notorious – during the First World War, when he had been imprisoned for his advocacy of pacifism. At that time he had been involved with the Union for Democractic Control. This had three main aims. First, to secure parliamentary control over foreign policy and prevent it being shaped in secret and forced upon the country as an accomplished fact. This was a response to Grey's unlikely agreement with the French before 1914, but was still deeply relevant to the cosy way policy was (and is) shaped. Second, to create an international organisation 'able and willing to secure obedience by force'. This was deeply objectionable both to the Government and to the out-and-out pacifists, but was seen by Russell as the best hope for peace. Third, passive resistance. 'If this were adopted deliberately by the will of the whole nation, with the same measure of courage and discipline which is now displayed in war,' wrote Russell in the *Atlantic Monthly*, 'it might achieve far more perfect protection for what is good in national life than armies and navies can ever achieve, without demanding the carnage and waste and welter of brutality involved in modern war.'[3] This theory had since been throughly tested and proved by Mahatma Gandhi.

All these aims were as relevant to the current situation as they had been forty-five years previously. The second had achieved a certain respectability, in that it resembled some of the ideas mooted during that period in 1946 and 1947 when international control of atomic energy had been under discussion at the UN. But the first and third were still utterly repugnant to the Government, and the third worrying also to those members of CND who thought the preservation of legitimacy was an important factor in the Campaign. Russell and his fellow-members of the Committee of 100 had no such reservations. Their position was succinctly expressed by the aged philosopher during his trial on the occasion of his being sent to prison once again, this time for seven days in September 1961: 'Non-violent civil disobedience was forced upon us by the fact that it was more fully reported than other methods of making the facts known, and that caused people to ask what had induced us to adopt such a course of action. We who are here accused are prepared to suffer imprisonment because we believe that this is the most effective way of working for the salvation of our country and the world. If you condemn us you will be helping our cause, and therefore humanity.'[4]

The activities of those who followed Russell to direct action were to ensure that the last years of CND's first incarnation were enlivened by a sputter of extramural sorties from which the movement's official leadership solemnly dissociated itself, but which achieved two important ends. This first was, of course, publicity. The second was a furious reaction on the part of the authorities so disproportionate to what had been done that it was clear they felt deeply threatened in some fundamental way.

The occasion of Russell's imprisonment arose from the first of these sorties. In June 1961, the Committee of 100 had applied for permission to use Trafalgar Square on 17 September for a meeting prior to a 'sit-down'. After a two-month delay, which ensured that Parliament would be in recess and so no discussion possible, the Ministry of Works refused the request – the first time such a request had been refused by the authorities since before the First World War. Russell encouraged supporters of the Committee to assemble in the Square anyway, and was imprisoned, along with thirty-one others. He and his wife got seven days; some of the others received two-month sentences. As a result of the publicity attending all this, the Committee's plans for 17 September became widely known. A great many people came to Trafalgar Square that day, despite the fact that permission had been refused. By 5 p.m., when the leaders of the

Committee of 100 came from the National Gallery into the Square, between five and seven thousand people were assembled inside it, and the surrounding streets were very crowded. By 5.30 the Square was fairly full; about five thousand people were sitting down, and as many again standing and watching. As time went on, spectators left and a core of activists remained. There were some arrests and some rough handling.

Just after midnight most people left the Square. About three hundred remained assembled round the plinth. They announced they were going to stay there until Russell was released from prison at ten the next morning. An official police statement said they could stay there all night if they wished. Then, at about twelve minutes past midnight, a new busload of police arrived, and set to. People were being dragged across the Square, others were dragged (according to the National Council for Civil Liberties official report on the incident) 'at the double, sometimes by one arm or both legs, across . . . to buses parked in the Strand. There were loud protests from bystanders in the streets, several of whom sat down in the road near the buses by way of protest. They were manhandled with similar vigour. Some of those arrested went on foot; they were, however, also made to run by the police, with their arms twisted behind their backs. . .'[5] The NCCL received forty-five letters containing allegations of police violence, of which thirty-one were detailed first-hand accounts.

Incidents of this kind are almost commonplace today. This was not so in the Britain of the early 1960s. It was particularly unusual for the police to deal so brutally with a literate, middle-class crowd who were not members of any prohibited organisation. What emerges time and again from the accounts of the brutality is astonishment at its disproportionate nature. What, after all, was happening? The crowd was in no way threatening. It was simply sitting about in a place where the public are liable to sit about anyway. Simply, there had been a quite arbitrary and exceptional ban on the assembly (and the ban had been extended, on the spot and at the last minute, for a further twenty-four hours). Clearly the sensible thing for the police to do would have been to ignore the whole thing. The situation would have been defused and the members of the Committee of 100 disappointed. But (because of the ban) they could not do this. The police were therefore placed in a ludicrous and embarrassing situation, and took it out on the demonstrators. But the reported over-reaction was such that there was clearly more to it than this.

The police in Britain have an apolitical tradition. They represent the rule of law, not the attempts of government or management to quell legally protesting citizenry. Their role is not to take sides (except against criminals) but to act as a buffer between warring parties, and so to preserve the peace.

This ideal position is not always easy to maintain. It is most threatened when the situation is ambiguous – as for instance when the police are ordered to break up demonstrations in which the government asserts that the demonstrators are acting illegally, while the latter maintain that they are within their rights. In recent years such situations have occurred fairly frequently – since World War II, most often in connection with causes supported by the Left, such as nuclear disarmament or the 1985 miners' strike. In such circumstances it is not unusual for those arrested to complain that they are treated with gratuitous brutality – far more than if they had been 'ordinary' criminals with whom the police, presumably, feel more at ease. One can only assume that the police feel uncomfortable in their newly politicised role, and take it out on those whom they perceive as having forced them into it.

It was not only in Britain that the questioning of nuclear policy caused embarrassment and over-reaction by the authorities. The next such occasion occurred just over a year after the Trafalgar Square sit-down, this time in the Federal Republic of Germany.

In September 1962, NATO held its autumn manoeuvres, Fallex 62. It so happened that this was the first NATO exercise to assume that World War III would begin with a nuclear attack on Europe. NATO's war began on the evening of 21 September, when a nuclear bomb exploded over a German air force base, followed by other nuclear attacks against NATO bases in the Federal Republic, England, Italy and Turkey. What happened next was revealed by the German weekly magazine *Der Spiegel* in its 10 October issue. 'The immediate retaliation by NATO did not . . . stop the Red attack. The East still had enough divisions and nuclear weapons to support the attack. After a few days large parts of England and the Federal Republic were totally destroyed. In both countries allowances were made for between ten and fifteen million dead. In the United States, which had been attacked in the meantime with a number of Soviet H-bombs, the losses were far greater. The chaos was unimaginable. . . The medical services broke down first. . . The provision of foodstuffs and the maintenance of vital industries and means of transport were no better. The Civil Defence measures were shown to be totally insufficient. It was impossible to control the streams of refugees. The telegraph and telephone system was very quickly out of order.

'The officials and spectators taking part in the manoeuvre . . . were shaken by the course of events. . .'[6]

The authorities' reaction to the publication of this information, some of which was reputedly classified 'cosmic secret' by NATO, pushed even the Cuban missile crisis off the front page in Germany. The police descended in the middle of the night on the houses of the paper's publisher, Rudolf Augstein, and its assistant editor, Dr Jakobi, and turned the houses upside-down in the search for secret material. Even the children were turfed out of bed so that their mattresses could be searched. Augstein was put in prison, and Jakobi was taken into 'interrogatory arrest'. The paper's military correspondent was arrested in Spain through Interpol. Two more journalists were eventually arrested, putting the total of Der Spiegel's staff in prison at five. The police took over the paper's offices, and were still there more than a month later, reputedly searching for evidence to bolster their case, and making Der Spiegel's continued production almost impossible.

In a country where the memories of Nazism were still relatively recent, such behaviour, quite apart from any question of immediate justice, carried disturbing overtones. The authorities' excuse for this astounding behaviour was that the article contained top NATO secrets, and that the securing and publication of these secrets involved 'treasonable acts'. In fact the paper's manager, Hans-Detlev Becker, who was also arrested, insisted that the piece had been cleared with the Ministry of Defence before publication. But it was known that the Defence Minister, Franz-Josef Strauss, hated Der Spiegel, which had consistently criticised his insistence that Germany should have nuclear weapons and accused him of authoritarianism and corruption.

The notion that this was a personal feud against Der Spiegel was given substance by the fact that, although the State Prosecutor's case was based largely on the accusation that the paper's correspondents had been bribing government servants, no official was arrested.

The *Spiegel* affair naturally caused more of a sensation in Germany than elsewhere, especially as the Cuban missile crisis was pre-occupying the rest of the world. The CND 1963 Easter march, however, revived flagging memories with a jolt – a nasty jolt for those British officials who had dismissed the original *Spiegel* article and insisted that they were still 'assessing' the information provided by Fallex.

The 1963 march was generally expected to be a low-key affair. Events had overtaken CND. Marching from Aldermaston, for the sixth year in succession, seemed no more than a reflex gesture. Lord Russell had resigned from the Committee of 100. So had Vanessa Redgrave, who said 'she did not think that what she ought to be doing now was preparing for demonstration after demonstration.'[7] Then, lifting the whole thing back on to the front pages, along came the 'Spies for Peace' – Britain's very own *Spiegel* affair.

On 11 April, the Thurday before the Aldermaston march was due to start, various leaders of CND received a strange document through the post. It did not contain any new 'cosmic secret' information but it did, according to angry officials, contain many 'serious breaches' of the Official Secrets Act – indeed, it was headed DANGER! OFFICIAL SECRET.

The document was six pages long, and it described in great detail some of Britain's plans for mobilising emergency services in the event of a nuclear attack. Undoubtedly its most famous revelation was the secret locations of regional underground headquarters in the emergency network – the Regional Seats of Government, or RSGs. On the back of the pamphlet was a map showing the exact location of one of the RSGs, with a suggestion that marchers could easily visit the site. (Many did.) The document also referred to Fallex 62 and the *Spiegel* affair, commenting that 'the British press wept crocodile tears about censorship over there, but has so far not said a word about the same exercise in Britain.' It revealed that during the exercise the chaos in England was every bit as great as that in Germany. Every hospital in southern England was destroyed or put out of action by fall-out, the death of doctors or lack of supplies. The communications system broke down and roads were choked. Gloucester, Oxford and Plymouth were eliminated by small bombs and London was paralysed. A lethal belt of radiation extended from the city as far as Windsor and three-quarters of the police in the southern region were killed, injured or suffered from radiation. Losses among the civilian population were assumed to be proportionally higher.

There was nothing in the pamphlet to identify the author or authors, and no indication of where it had been printed. It did not purport to be the work of anyone in CND or the Committee of 100, although the author(s) clearly sympathised with the movement's aims. The authorities said that details of the emergency plans were so complete that they must have been obtained from secret files, and there was one clue – a sentence reading: 'There is no defence against nuclear war. At least one occupant of one RSG is convinced that the deterrent is quite futile.' It went on: 'This document is an official secret. Secrets are kept from you because you may be a spy. Not for Russia, but for all people everywhere. We are spies for peace. We have decided to publish an official secret. All we have is a voice. We have done what we can. You have a voice too. If you spread this story as widely and as quickly as you can, you will stop the authorities ever hiding it again. A secret has escaped. Give it a good run before they catch it. Read it. Discuss it. Hand it round. Reprint it. There are thousands more secrets in captivity. This is not the only one we shall release. Do you know a secret?'

The leaders of CND of course dissociated themselves from the action. 'We would not condone action of this kind,' said one of them, Mr Anthony Greenwood, MP. But the Spies for Peace (none of whom has ever been identified) had done something very important. They had identified what was to be one of the main battlegrounds of the peace movement: the battle against government secrecy, that obsessive secretiveness which was one of the earliest legacies of nuclear power and whose corrosive effect on civil liberties leads to what has been dubbed 'The Nuclear State'.

7

Fallout

In the autumn of 1962 the Cuban missile crisis terrified the world and its leaders, and in the summer of 1963 the Partial Test-Ban Treaty between the United States and the Soviet Union was concluded.

Obviously the first of these events – the terror felt by both decision-makers and the general public during the crisis, and the profound relief when war was averted – played no small part in creating the frame of mind which made the second possible. A relevant question for movements such as CND was – had they played any part in these momentous events? The answer seemed to be – in the first, none at all: members of peace movements, even in America and certainly in Britain, were as impotent as everyone else. And in the second – possibly, but only indirectly, by acting as a focus for worries largely connected with the side-effects of nuclear weapons, rather than the weapons themselves.

The history of atomic energy, in both its military and civilian applications, has to a large extent been a history of nasty surprises. The first of these to catch the public imagination in a big way was strontium 90.

Clement Attlee, talking about what was known in 1945, said: 'We knew nothing whatever at that time about the genetic effects of an atomic explosion. I knew nothing about fall-out and all the rest of what emerged after Hiroshima. As far as I know, President Truman and Winston Churchill knew nothing of these things either, nor did Sir John Anderson, who coordinated research on our side. Whether the scientists directly concerned knew, or guessed, I do not know. But if they did, then, so far as I am aware, they said nothing of it to those who had to make the decision.'[1]

This was not strictly true. By 1945, both the leading scientists and some politicians knew a good deal about the general effects of radiation and radioactivity, but considered them secondary in military terms to the enormous explosive power of the bomb. (Oppenheimer had discussed the possibility of using radioactive material against the Germans, but this idea was abandoned.) Passing mention had been made of possible genetic effects, but little was known of this. Attlee himself knew very little because until he went to Potsdam in July 1945, he was barely aware of the bomb's existence.

How much people will admit, or allow themselves to admit, of what they know, is of course a very different matter. General Groves, testifying before a Senate committee just after the War, said that he understood that death from radiation was 'a very pleasant death'.[2] But nobody believed that for very long, and, as we have seen, by the mid-fifties the amount of radioactive debris caused by bomb tests in peacetime – never mind what might happen in a war – was causing concern. The tests, however, went inexorably on. The Princeton physicist Freeman Dyson, temporarily employed in 1962 at the then newly established Arms Control and Disarmament Agency, plotted a diagram of the tests up to that date. 'As soon as the diagram was finished, the situation became clear. The curve of cumulative bomb totals was an almost exact exponential, all the way from 1945 to 1962, with a doubling time of three years. A simple explanation suggested itself for this doubling every three years. It takes roughly three years to plan and carry out a bomb test. Suppose that every completed bomb test raises two new questions which have to be answered by two new bomb tests three years later. Then the exponential curve is explained.'[3]

By the late fifties, there can be little doubt that it was this aspect of nuclear weapons, rather than the military dangers, which was most worrying to the public. The fact that strontium travels from grass through cows into milk and so into children, where it acts in the same way as calcium, concentrating in the bones, where it may cause cancer, was particularly emotive. In Britain, the *Observer* newspaper, reflecting public concern, published in November 1961 a 'Q and A on Fall-out and the Family', where expert answers were given to questions frequently asked in letters received by the paper. Examples were:

Q: 'I have a baby under one year old. Should I cut down his fresh milk?'

A: 'No. If the Russian bomb tests had continued at a very rapid rate a dangerous amount of radioactive iodine might have appeared in milk. But the tests have now stopped, and the iodine levels are now falling.'

Q: 'But even if the risk is small, surely I ought to make every possible effort to protect myself and my children – perhaps by emigrating somewhere where there is less fall-out?'

A: 'The risk you would be running away from would be of the order of one in millions, and by moving you would affect your chances only minutely. . .'

Q: 'Then what are all the protests about?'

A: 'The protests are quite legitimate because although the chances of the bomb tests affecting any particular individual are very small, the world population as a whole will almost certainly be affected. . .'[4]

Such fundamental and universal worries enabled appeals to stop the bomb tests to be put in ways which even the most conservative might find hard to resist. George Meany, the veteran president of the American Federation of Labor, testifying before the Senate Foreign Relations Committee during the Partial Test-Ban Treaty ratification hearings, used this technique to optimum effect. 'He fulminated for fifteen minutes against the Russians, describing the contempt and distrust with which the honest laborers of America regarded the deceitful Communist negotiators. Then, right at the end of his speech, he came on with his punch line. But, he said, the honest laborers of America also have to think of their wives and children. They have to protect their wives and children from the poison that falls from the sky as a result of bomb tests. So for the sake of their wives and children, and in spite of their distrust and contempt for the Communists, the honest laborers of America support the treaty.'[5]

For some purists, the confusion of motives involved in the strontium 90 campaign was disturbing. S. A. Goudsmit, a veteran of Los Alamos, expressed these worries in a letter to the *Bulletin of the Atomic Scientists*. 'Whenever I dare to point out that smog, food additives, fast-moving vehicles, and other man-made nuisances are likely to be more lethal than fallout, I am treated to the usual explanation of why fallout is different,' he wrote plaintively. '. . .The underlying reason why the fallout foes wish the bomb tests stopped is the hope that it will

56

be a first step towards preventing a nuclear war and perhaps even opening the way to the abolition of all nuclear warfare. I fully subscribe to this premise but fear that the fallout controversy deflects attention from the real aim, disarmament. I believe that the fallout issue is a new example of the old and unsuccessful tactic of using fear and horror to put a perfectly acceptable idea across.'[6]

Between 1958 and 1960 there was a three-year moratorium on nuclear testing; in 1961 and 1962, the US and the Soviet Union exploded more bombs than ever before. After the Cuban missile crisis, when the terror of nuclear war was brought home to the world to add to the terror of poisoning through radioactive bomb-test products, it was clear that the time was ripe for real negotiations to lessen the dangers.

Ever since the late 1950s there had been an active lobby in the US pushing for a comprehensive test-ban treaty – an agreement to stop all further nuclear tests. Had this been achieved, it would have meant the end of the nuclear arms race in any real sense, since tests are about improvements, modifications and new ideas. Lobbying against this was intense, not only from the weapons laboratories and the military (and especially from Edward Teller: 'I am still against the test-ban,' he reiterated in a recent interview) – but also from those scientists who were involved with non-military applications of nuclear power such as Project Plowshare, in which nuclear power was to be used as a blasting agent for dams and harbours, and Project Orion, which was for sending a nuclear-powered space-ship around the solar system. But by 1963 there was enough political will on both sides to overcome most of these objections. That summer Averell Harriman, the American Secretary of State, went over to Moscow to negotiate the treaty. It was a compromise. Nuclear explosions were prohibited in the atmosphere, in outer space or under water; or in any environment if the explosion were to cause radioactive debris to be deposited outside the territorial limits of the state under whose jurisdiction or control the explosion was conducted. The effect of the treaty was to push weapons tests underground. There was a hitch in the talks when the Americans, with Project Plowshare in mind, tried to insist that above-ground tests should be allowed. But the Russians were not having that on any account. Finally the Americans gave way, and the Partial Test-Ban Treaty was signed. However, it was only signed by three nuclear weapons powers – the US, the USSR, and the UK. France and China refused to sign (though France stopped atmospheric tests in 1975). The agreement that had been reached was better than nothing, but it was less than satisfactory to serious disarmers. Goudsmit was right: the only anti-bomb lobby which could be much satisfied was that which was worried only by fall-out. A compromised approach had led to a compromised achievement. The bomb-tests had been banished underground, but they went on. The only nuclear projects genuinely killed by the partial test-ban were those such as Orion and Plowshare.

What had also been killed, of course, was the impetus behind the anti-nuclear movement. A substantial gesture had been made, the two sides seemed to be on better terms, the bomb had vanished underground and the public felt free to think about other things. The eagerness and thoroughness with which this happened – reflecting people's deep desire not to have to think about these things – can be seen if, to take one example, one rereads a book first published in 1964: Tom Stonier's *Nuclear Disaster*. In it he discussed all the issues – including an adumbration of the nuclear winter – which were hailed as new and devastating revelations when they resurfaced in the 1980s, for example in Jonathan Schell's *The Fate of the Earth*.

Just why an idea should sink like a stone one year and take off twenty years later is a subject to which we shall return. But the relief with which the authorities viewed the sinking of this particular idea, or group of ideas, can be seen by the alacrity and determination with which they prevented any real attempt to help them resurface – most notoriously by the BBC's banning, in 1964, of Peter Watkins's film *The War Game*.

Watkins was a director who specialised in super-realism. His previous film, *Culloden*, had captured in a unique way the sense of what it felt like to participate in hand-to-hand battle. History had come to life. Now he applied the same techniques to a depiction of Britain after a nuclear attack. The action took place during and after the dropping of a bomb near Canterbury. What made the film uniquely powerful and moving was the way in which it showed just how every small detail of normal life would be transformed by the grim new reality. The mode of the film is bleak horror rather than sustained melodrama. Its impact comes from its absolute inducement of participation – the sense that, for the duration, not only the actors but the spectators are part of the action. There can be little doubt that had *The War Game* been shown when it was made, the subject of

58

nuclear disarmament would not have slid gently out of public consciousness.

The Chairman of the BBC's Board of Governors at this time was Lord Normanbrook, who as Cabinet Secretary ten years earlier had been instrumental in preventing any information about Britain's then nuclear programme from leaking into the public domain. It was he who insisted that the film be viewed by, and the matter referred to, the Government, who were – as he of course knew they would be – appalled at the prospect of its showing. Even Sir Hugh Greene, one of the strongest and most liberal Directors-General the BBC ever had, could not stand out against this pressure. The film was banned on the grounds that it was too horrific and that people could not cope with such stuff in their sitting-rooms. As the years went on and interest in the subject reawakened, the BBC justified its continued refusal to show the film on the grounds that, because of changes in policies and social conditions since it was made, it was now out of date. When, in 1985, it was finally shown, Peter Watkins collected an award as best television director of the year – twenty years too late.

The ban caused a furore at the time and the film has been shown repeatedly since in various clubs and political groups, where its impact is invariably devastating. But furore and club showings are no substitute for national television exposure, as Normanbrook well knew.

What the ban showed was that, firstly, the subject, test-ban or no test-ban, was still a delicate one which governments did not want reawakened. And secondly, that CND had, in its years of campaigning, touched some very sore spots over which the authorities now hoped to spread the healing balm of oblivion. Out of sight, out of mind, was their fervent wish, as the sixties drew on. And, up to a point – in Britain, at least – that hope was fulfilled.

8

The Sixties

A great deal of soul-searching went on over the decline of CND after the early sixties. Did it happen because of the Partial Test-Ban Treaty? Or because of the split over Direct Action? Or because public interest is fickle? These and many other reasons have been adduced, and probably all of them are right.

But in a sense the very concentration on these questions may be part of the answer to them. For the decline of CND by no means meant that the peace movement, or, more narrowly, the anti-nuclear movement, was finished. What CND had done was to show that, even in so apolitical a country as Britain, a mass political movement could be set in motion on the single issue of nuclear weapons. This particular manifestation was now played out, but the action had not ended. It had simply moved elsewhere.

By the time CND died down, the anti-nuclear movement was active all over Europe. In 1962, twelve countries sent delegates to a meeting of the European Federation against Nuclear Arms in Copenhagen. In 1964, the establishment of the NATO multilateral force giving the West German military control of nuclear weapons set 100,000 demonstrators marching at Easter for a nuclear-free Europe, followed by a 'Europe week' in June. But these European manifestations by no means represented all that was happening. The real action now was in America.

In the USA, where – unlike Britain – single issues are the stuff of politics, events conspired to keep the nuclear issue and others related to it continuously before the public. There, a whole new set of political techniques was devised, and issues drawn together, which (as it turned out) would be transplanted to the forefront of European consciousness twenty years later.

If the most important condition for the success of a protest movement is that its opponent should be clearly defined, then the United States during the fifties was designed to nurture the most successful protest movements ever – all battling against the activities of Senator Joe McCarthy and his House Un-American Activities Committee (HUAC).

From the outset, atomic activities had been at the centre of this Committee's scrutiny. The shadow of Klaus Fuchs had fallen across the atomic scientists. Opposition to the H-bomb, even under the most elevated official auspices, had destroyed Robert Oppenheimer's public career. And not only Oppenheimer: any nuclear scientist with faintly radical leanings was liable to find himself under the scrutiny of HUAC. The situation was extraordinarily ironic. If the nuclear programme was to go ahead the skills of these men were desperately needed; but they were at the same time objects of profound suspicion. Dr E. U. Condon, who was under constant scrutiny by HUAC between 1947 and 1954, during which time he was head of the National Bureau of Standards, and whose resignation from this post was forced in 1955 despite his having had his security clearance confirmed four times in HUAC hearings, described a typical occurrence from those years: 'I was cleared from July 1954 to October 1954. During that period some navy people called to see me with an urgent problem on the development of a radome for a guided missile. It was highly secret, but I was cleared for it. By the time we had the development models made my clearance had been suspended "pending further consideration" as Secretary Thomas put it. Some of our cleared young men tried to deliver the radomes but found the navy men in such a state of panic that they would not accept them! A few weeks later . . . they regained their courage and sheepishly asked to have the radomes. They were tested and found to be good and are now in production. Detailed problems about them come up from time to time but I am not allowed to help in their solution.'[1]

Condon, it will be noted, was not even working against nuclear weapons – all he asked was to be allowed to work on them in peace. This privilege was denied him apparently on the grounds that he had once been interested in the American-Soviet Science Society, an organisation interested in scientific exchange and the fostering of translation and wider distribution of Russian scientific literature in America – an activity which at the time Condon was speaking, just after the launch of Sputnik, was the object of crash programmes throughout the States.

The Senate Internal Security Committee produced a report on the Pugwash organisation which was magisterially shredded by Bertrand Russell: '[the report] regards it as self-evident that any person in the West who wishes to diminish East-West tension must be actuated by pro-Communist bias: that in any more or less friendly contact between any Communist and any non-Communist, the Communist must be capable of outwitting the non-Communist, however great might be the ability of the latter; that any Communist participant in Pugwash Conferences must only express the policy of his Government; but that, nevertheless, in spite of Pugwash pronouncements in favour of peace, which Communists have signed, the Russian Government is bent on war... The whole tone of the report is to the effect that the wicked Russians praise peace, while all patriotic Americans praise war. Any unprejudiced person, reading the Report and believing it, would inevitably be driven to the support of Russia.'[2]

It took a great deal of courage and an unassailable position for a scientist to stand out successfully against this kind of pressure. The outstanding example of one who did was Linus Pauling, who had in 1954 won the Nobel Prize for Chemistry to the general gratification and applause of Americans who hailed him as perhaps the greatest native-born American scientist. In 1957, Pauling gave an address at Washington University, St Louis, on the subject of 'Science and the Modern World'. In it he discussed the role of abnormal molecules in producing hereditary diseases. 'I mentioned that the bomb tests now being made are increasing the number of bad genes, and are probably also causing people to die of leukemia and other diseases. Then I said that Dr Albert Schweitzer has said that "A humanitarian is a man who believes that no human being should be sacrificed to a project." I continued in the following way: "I am a humanitarian. I believe that no human being should be sacrificed to a project; and in particular I believe that no human being should be sacrificed to the project of perfecting nuclear weapons that could kill hundreds of millions of human beings, could devastate this beautiful world in which we live." '[3]

The enthusiasm with which this address was received decided Pauling to prepare an appeal that could be signed by American scientists, an idea that had arisen the day before when he was telling the chairman of the committee that had invited him to St Louis, Dr Barry Commoner, what he was going to say.

The appeal was mimeographed later that evening, and some letters typed, which Pauling sent to a few other scientists asking if they would join him in making the appeal. Within a week he had had answers from 26; on 22 May a few hundred copies of the appeal were sent to people in various universities and laboratories around the United States and, by 2 June, Pauling had received 2000 signatures of American scientists at his home in Pasadena.

At this point Pauling was asked by a reporter if he would like to see scientists from other countries associate themselves with his appeal; of course, he said. A month later, he received a letter from Belgium in which 40 scientists from the Free University of Brussels appended their signatures to the appeal. More and more such communications arrived from different places, and by September, Pauling decided to internationalise the project in earnest. He employed a private secretary and sent out 500 letters to scientists in different parts of the world – some he knew, some whose names were known to him through their authorship of scientific papers, some selected from reference books. These 500 letters produced 7500 signatures – a total of 9500 signatures altogether. The appeal, with its signatures, was then sent as a petition to Dag Hammarskjöld, the Secretary-General of the United Nations. It was this petition which first brought the issue of fall-out effects to the public's attention, resulting in that mushrooming of indignation which later led to the Partial Test-Ban Treaty.

Not unexpectedly, Pauling's doings aroused great suspicion in certain circles. It was assumed at once that he was merely the front for some nefarious unnamed organisation. President Eisenhower, to whom a copy of the appeal had been sent, with a letter, reputedly commented to this effect; when asked about this by James Reston of the *New York Times* he said, 'I said that there does seem to be some organisation behind it. I didn't say a wicked organisation.' Fulton Lewis, a syndicated columnist, had no such reservations. He clearly thought Pauling sinister in the extreme. On 12 February 1958 he wrote, 'Which organisation or individuals helped Dr Pauling in his worldwide operation? Also, such a petition costs money; lots of it.

Experts tell me that the expense would average $10 per signature. It is certainly not amiss for a congressional committee to inquire who raised the necessary $100,000.' To which Pauling replied, 'Who are Mr Lewis's experts? They seem not to understand this issue – they greatly overestimated the cost of getting the signatures of scientists to an appeal urging an international agreement to stop bomb tests. It was about three cents per signature, instead of ten dollars. However, I have been told by people with experience in gathering signatures by mail that a yield of one signature in ten letters is not unusual in such a campaign. The yield that I obtained, 15 signatures per letter, was accordingly 150 times the ordinary yield. . .'[4]

Inevitably Pauling was hauled before HUAC, where a commentator for the *Bulletin of the Atomic Scientists* remarked that he seemed insouciant to the point of apparently rather enjoying himself – and discomfiting the Committee and their counsel, a Mr Sourwine.[5] But there were few scientists with the status (let alone the tenacity) to pursue something of this sort in the way Pauling did. Pauling resigned from Caltech to join the Center for the Study of Democratic Institutions in Santa Barbara, where he could devote himself full-time to peace work. He was a celebrated man near the end of his career (he had taught at Caltech since 1922), and he retained the clout of celebrity (he won the Nobel Peace Prize in 1963) while being able to continue his work away from the laboratory. But most scientists need laboratories, and they are usually to be found in universities, which in turn are easy targets for government pressure of one kind or another. The heady post-war days of the FAS had gone. A new initiative was needed, just as it was needed in Europe.

With the advent of the Kennedy Administration, it seemed for a while as though that initiative might come from within government itself. For some time the scientists attached to the Democratic Advisory Council on Science and Technology had been proposing what they called a Peace Agency. This was to be funded to the tune of half a billion dollars a year and was to be a sort of mirror-image of the RAND organisation. RAND (Research And Development) was (and is) a think-tank working mainly for the armed forces and the Pentagon. The new agency would perform an equivalent service in the cause of peace and disarmament. It was also to intervene in Cold War policy-making, putting the arms-control case. It was to be a 'countering force' to what the outgoing President had identified as 'the military-industrial complex' under the checks-and-balances system that operates throughout American government.

When Kennedy became President in 1962, one of his first acts was to form the Arms Control and Disarmament Agency. ACDA was to be the channel through which the Partial Test-Ban Treaty was negotiated – but, not unexpectedly, conservatives regarded it with intense suspicion from the start. Congress, having refused the President's suggested name of 'Peace and Disarmament Agency', slapped a ceiling of ten million dollars on ACDA's budget; that budget was 1/1700 of that of the Department of Defense. As for its personnel – who were they to be? Robert A. Lovett, former Secretary of Defense, remarked that it would be deplorable if it turned into 'a Mecca for a wide variety of screwballs. It would be a great pity to have this launched and then become a sort of bureau of beatniks.' The military, meanwhile, were even more wary of the new agency. One original idea had been that ACDA should operate out of the White House as an executive arm of the President. The military were all against this. General Lyman Lemnitzer, testifying before the House Armed Services Committee in 1961, was particularly concerned that ACDA's recommendations should not go to the President direct, but should be transmitted through the National Security Council, 'where Defense Department and Joint Chiefs of Staff have an opportunity to express their views.' A campaign originating mostly in the conservative South and West was mounted against ACDA; it was said to have more money behind it than the Agency itself disposed of. Many Congressmen reported that they received more mail on this subject than on any other.[6]

It was clear, then, that ACDA, however well-intentioned, would never do the nuclear disarmament movement's job for it. It might be, and was, a clearing-house for ideas, and if any of them were ever put into practice it would be through ACDA, but that in itself was not enough. Public pressure was needed, as always in politics, but especially in American politics.

But what sort of movement, what sort of pressure, would this be? Bertrand Russell, writing in 1959, had commented that 'It is surprising and somewhat disappointing that movements aiming at the prevention of nuclear war are regarded throughout the West as Left-Wing movements or as inspired by some "ism" which is repugnant to a majority of ordinary people. It is not in this way that opposition to nuclear warfare should be conceived. It should be conceived rather on the analogy of a sanitary measure against epidemics.' Russell cited the Black Death. 'But nuclear war is much more dangerous than the Black Death, over which all nations would of course cooperate now.'[7]

Russell was writing from his own experience, which was mainly European, and what he said was undoubtedly true of the European anti-nuclear movement. But it was not necessarily the best way to look at what was happening during the sixties and seventies in the United States. It was true that, during the McCarthy era, anyone betraying worries about the nuclear arms programme was liable to be dubbed a commie traitor. But that was now past, and what obtained more in the sixties and seventies was what might be termed 'lifestyle' politics. Politics could be seen as being composed of infinite numbers of single issues, and a person's politics might be deduced from the issues with which he or she chose to become involved. Thus if a person was into health foods, against cigarette smoking, had long hair, smoked dope and wanted it legalised, was into women's liberation (and so, if female, against bras, 'straight' clothes and other attributes of the traditional feminine lifestyle), it could fairly be assumed that such a person would also be anti-war. The environmental movement was marked by an environmental lifestyle; a whole publishing industry sprang up concerning itself with domes, energy conservation, solar power, wind power, hydroponics, the 'French Intensive' method of gardening vegetables, compost, garbage, and a host of related issues. People who took up these interests could also fairly be assumed to be against 'the system'.

This may sound trivial, but the point is real. Where a European observes a personal eccentricity and sees it just as that, an American looks for an indicator and makes his assumptions from there. Among the many reasons for this is, in my view, an essential difference between the American and the European – especially the British – view of politics. In Britain, there is politics and there is life – two quite separate things, the one possibly, if you are that way inclined, forming a part of the other. But in America, this separation is quite unreal. In the absence of theoretical party politics on the European model, politics is a series of issues – taxation, health care, education, pollution, equal opportunities or whatever – and of these issues life is composed. The personal, to take the women's movement phrase, is political. The issues are the politics. Under these circumstances, a person's stand on one issue is reasonably seen as an indicator of his stand on a host of others. Thus, just as Bertrand Russell's view of what the nuclear disarmament movement should be was quintessentially British, Paul Goodman's view of what it should become in the 1960s was quintessentially American: 'The peace movement is at present astoundingly negative: "strike for peace" means merely "refuse the Cold War." The most popular slogan is Ban the Bomb, and there is a rising realization that Peace Must Come from the People. But the idea of positively waging peace – in acts of community-forming, new culture, political reconstruction, economic reconversion – seems not yet to take hold of popular fancy.'[8]

Despite Goodman's impatience, such deep changes of viewpoint do not spring fully-formed into the general consciousness. The new politics he was advocating developed gradually in the United States during the sixties and seventies. Thus, when a commentator remarked in 1964 (referring to the peace movement's dilemma because it had been making dire predictions for so long and none of them had come true) that 'Many of the peace movement militants are now in civil rights, as if to prove that either the need or the results are greater there',[9] this could be seen not as an abdication, but simply as another part of the same politics.

For, even if it did not seem to Paul Goodman that this integration existed, it certainly did seem like that to people such as the members of the House Un-American Activities Committee. McCarthyism had not altogether died out with the eponymous Senator, even if some of its more outrageous manifestations had done so. HUAC saw, as it had always seen, the whole brew – peace activists, civil rights, the emerging feminist and environmental movements – as parts of a lumpen radical carbuncle, indistinguishably undesirable. Their vision of a general conspiracy, by producing a common enemy, helped produce the fusion it pictured; and the tactics and thinking that were worked out during the dangerous days of sixties and seventies America enormously affected events and connections in Europe in the eighties.

An early example of this could be seen in the HUAC questioning of fifteen members of Women Strike for Peace, or WISP, an American group founded by Mrs Dagmar Wilson. The group came into being, in November 1961, in a kind of 'chain reaction' – to quote Barbara Deming, an early exponent of the new politics, and a participant in WISP. A group of women in Washington had announced they were on strike against nuclear policy, and demanded the resumption of disarmament negotiations; whereupon, right across the country, other groups of women announced that they, too, would join the strike. Nothing could have been milder or less inflammatory than their Declaration, which called upon both sides to reconvene negotiations, to allow inspection, to budget for a conversion to a peacetime economy, and so on. WISP made suggestions, such as that both sides should immediately destroy the means of launching missiles, so reducing the risk of accidental war; and they resolved that, on the first day of every month, 'a committee of women in many nations will call upon their governments to ask for a report of progress towards a world disarmed'. This, apparently, was enough to alarm HUAC. In January, 1963, the women were subpoenaed to appear before it.

What was interesting about this occasion was the deep discrepancy it revealed between the world-view of the politicians and that of these perfectly ordinary women. Nowhere was this revealed more clearly than in the questions put to the women with the utmost solemnity by Counsel: 'Did you then . . . have you recently operated a mimeograph machine?. . .' 'This news item reports that a peace group met at the Unitarian Church hall and planned a theatre party. . . Did you prepare the press releases and make them available to the press?'[10] Not surprisingly, the most usual response to such questions was uncontrollable laughter. The members of the committee were discomfited in other ways, too. From the second day onwards each witness was greeted at the stand by a sympathiser bearing a large bouquet. Russell Baker wrote in the *New York Times*: 'The three luckless politicians watched the procession of gardenias, carnations and roses with the resigned looks of men aware that they were already liable to charges of being against housewives, children and peace, and determined not to get caught coming out against flowers.'[11]

It was clear from the nature of the questioning and the responses it evoked that the members of the Committee and the women before them lived in parallel worlds which never could meet, but which merely suffered the misfortune of happening to find themselves sharing a planet. The Chairman of the Committee, Mr Doyle, used certain portentous phrases – ' "excessive desire for peace" impeding "adequate defense preparations," sapping "national strength," serving the "aggressive plans of world communism". . .'.[12] But these had nothing to do with the women's life, nor with why they were there. The first witness, Blanche Posner, spoke for them all when she said,

68

'You don't understand the nature of this movement. It was motivated by mothers' love for their children. When they set their breakfast on the table, they see not wheaties and milk but strontium 90 and iodine 131 and they fear for their health and lives.' Another woman described how, during the Cuba crisis, her daughter had brought her best friend home from school with her because they wanted to die together.[13] HUAC's view was that the women, unfamiliar as they were with the intricacies of government, should leave these things to those who knew best and not meddle, or they might land themselves, all unwittingly, in more trouble than they bargained for. The women's view was that these men, who knew nothing about life, were simply not fit to be left with decisions which so deeply affected everyone's lives. As Barbara Deming put it, 'It has not dawned on them that the rapidly altering nature of the world about us has drained certain words of all former meaning: that the word "strength", for example, is meaningless when one speaks of weapons which, if we used them, would ensure our destruction – the mere testing of which damages us. When they think of testing – on our part, that is – they just think automatically: necessary to preserve that "freedom" for which Americans have always been willing to lay down their lives; and they are hypnotized by these words. Whereas the women see the cold fact that we are now willing to lay down our children's lives, and are already doing so.'[14] This was not just about the bomb. It was about feminism and the right of women to impose their specific world view in hitherto male preserves. It was the beginning of the road which led to Greenham Common.

9

Waging Peace

Although the members of HUAC and the participants in WISP inhabited different political worlds, the fact was that this reflected more on the antediluvian nature of HUAC than anything outlandishly advanced in WISP. For although both WISP and the active Women's Section of CND presaged the later involvement of the women's movement in the anti-nuclear movement of the 1980s, in that they all participated in the hope that the essential sanity of the women's world-view would prevail over the destructive madness of the men's, they were still very much of their own political time – that is, the time before Betty Friedan opened the flood-gates of the Women's Liberation movement with the publication of *The Feminine Mystique* in 1963. There was nothing particularly revolutionary about WISP. Unlike its feminist counterparts in the 1980s, it was not even to the left of the spectrum of organisations which comprised the American peace movement during the 1950s and 1960s.

The American movement at that time was contained within a dozen or so organisations. About half of these emerged after World War I and had survived to take up the new fight. These included the Women's International League for Peace and Freedom, the Quaker American Friends Service Committee, the War Resisters League and the Fellowship of Reconciliation. The other half had emerged during the Cold War: the United Nations Association for the United States, the United World Federalists, the National Committee for a Sane Nuclear Policy (SANE), the Committee for Non-Violent Resistance

(CNVR), Women Strike for Peace, and various student peace groups. These effectively spanned the liberal/radical spectrum. To the right were UNA and UWF, more critical of Russia than the US, and advocating a stronger United Nations leading to an eventual world state; in the centre were SANE, WISP, WILPF, critical of both sides, working towards general and complete disarmament. To the left were the religious pacifists such as the American Friends Service Committee, who advocated pacifism and unilateral American nuclear disarmament; and to the left again, those pacifists who operated from a religious-pacifist base but were working towards a utopian socialism to be achieved through sweeping changes in the social order. These included CNVR, the Fellowship of Reconciliation and the War Resisters League.

Many of the activities of these organisations were well within the normal spectrum of accepted political protest. A special issue of *New University Thought* devoted to the anti-nuclear movement in spring 1962 included (as well as historical and descriptive articles on such topics as the psychology of violence, civil defence in schools, the history and economics of disarmament, a 1961 peace walk) a section on the politics of peace. This included an article by a congressman about peace politics at the local level; questions for Congressional candidates – how to influence a Congressman; how to organise a speakers bureau; the Gradualist approach to peace; and how to organise a peace walk.

All these were activities which anyone could combine with their everyday life, and many did. Other exploits were more spectacular. On Good Friday 1962, *Sanity* (the CND publication) announced that the American Committee for Nonviolent Action was proposing to sail a boat into the Christmas Island testing area. The idea was that the American Government would then have to cancel the tests, postpone them until lack of supplies forced the crew to sail out, arrest or remove the crew knowing that this was probably illegal (legal action after previous anti-test sailings had ended with the regulations shutting off test areas being held invalid by the US courts) or go on with the tests knowing that the crewmen could be killed or seriously injured. The question then posed by the CNVA was, 'If you cannot bear to destroy four or five people, how can you contemplate the effects of nuclear war?'

But perhaps the most spectacular of all the American anti-bomb

71

movement's activities was the San Francisco to Moscow peace walk. This started in December 1960, and lasted ten months. Such a phrase trips neatly off the page: its real enormity can only be taken in by recalling some of the marchers' daily experiences. For example, just as they were approaching the very last stage – from the Polish border to Moscow, on 15 September 1961 – they heard that the Russians had resumed bomb testing and that their time in the USSR had been cut from six to three weeks. Regina Fischer and Cyril Pustan, who had met on the march and married on their return, described those weeks: 'Since the distance from the border of Russia to Moscow was so great (1054 km, 658 miles) and we had only three instead of six weeks to do it in, it became necessary to work out a shift system, somewhat similar to one we used for a short time in the wide western expanses in the United States, only more intensive.

'At first the Russians insisted we must stay together as a group, as we had actually agreed to do prior to our coming. To meet this requirement, and at the same time cover the mileage, meant that all the walkers had to get up at 4.45 a.m., eat and get out on the road, there to remain until perhaps 10 p.m. in order to be able to say honestly that the entire distance had actually been walked by one part of the team. Soon the two buses accompanying us began to look like ambulances. While part of the team walked, the others lay on seats and floors trying to catch up on a few hours' sleep until their turn to relieve the others. Evening meetings and entertainments kept the walkers going until 2 or 3 a.m. and some hardly bothered to undress before they reeled into bed.

'Soon the walkers began dropping like flies. Picked up by ambulances they were being taken to hospital with exhaustion, indigestion, and general disintegration. In alarm, the Russians called an emergency meeting with the group. They tried to dissuade the walkers, urging that they walk their usual approximate 40 km (25 miles) each day as a single group and then take the bus the rest of the way to their destination for the night. In vain they pointed out that much of the route to Moscow lay through sparsely inhabited swamp land and forest. The walkers remained determined – a walk was a walk and it must be walked. The Russians shook their heads over this, to them, quixotic attitude and gave in. Thereafter they cooperated in every way possible with a three-shift system asked for by the team, starting at 3 a.m. and finishing at about 8 p.m., enabling the team to complete the walk to Moscow on foot.'[1] The highlight of their time in

72

Moscow was a meeting with Mrs Khruschev at the House of Friendship. The team was impressed: 'No make-up, no Paris gown or foundation, just a dark dress, her hair in simple style. She was friendly and simple, the kind of woman you would go to for encouragement and advice.'[2]

The peace walkers took their leave of Mrs Khruschev in September 1961; that autumn the Russians resumed bomb tests after a three-year moratorium. Not long after HUAC attacked the WISP women (their interrogations before the committee took place in January 1963), the negotiations which led to the Partial Test-Ban Treaty were in train. Such concatenations seem designed to convey, in the clearest possible way, the gulf between the march of world events and the attempts of private individuals to influence them. And of course after the Treaty was signed the ground was cut from beneath the feet of the American anti-nuclear movement, as it was from its European equivalents.

But the domestic political situation in the United States at that time was radically different from that in Europe. During the late sixties and early seventies little was happening on the European domestic front to stir the political imagination. There were flurries of activity, such as the May events in Paris in 1968, but generally those members of the politically concerned middle classes who had formed the backbone of the anti-bomb movement relapsed into invisibility. In America, however, they turned their attention to other, more compelling political foci, notably Black civil rights, the Vietnam War and the pollution of the environment. During the sixties and seventies, political issues literally came home to millions of households across the United States.

And here we return to Paul Goodman's view of politics. For it was not merely the case that people who were concerned about one of these issues were also frequently concerned about the others as well. It was also true that, for many of them, the issues were indissolubly joined. It was a question of a different vision of the world. A concrete example of this is given by Barbara Deming. She took part in a peace walk through Mississippi, which was also part of the Southern heartland where segregation was strongest. Both blacks and whites took part in the walk. When night came most of the blacks left; the whites, with one black friend, were to spend the night in 'a little one-room Negro church by the side of the road, way out "nowhere" between towns.' Soon they were woken by the sound of rocks hitting the building, and after a while went outside and persuaded the rock-throwers to come and talk. 'They talked for a good while, and finally they said that well, they might perhaps agree with some of the things we said about war and peace, but they couldn't understand our walking around with a nigger, and all sleeping in the same building with him. And then one of them asked the time-worn question: "Would you let a nigger marry your sister?" The question was posed to Sam Savage, who is a Southerner himself. When he answered that yes, he would; the decision would, after all, be hers to make – they exclaimed in sudden anger and disgust: well, he was no real Southerner then, and there was no use talking about anything further; and they stamped off into the dark. At which point, one might have said that the advice we had been given before starting out on the walk had now been proved to be correct: the two issues of race relations and of war and peace could not be discussed together. However, there is a final chapter to this story. After a short time, the young men returned, wanting to talk further. The talk this time went on until the one who had done the most arguing remarked that they must be up early to work and had better get some sleep. But would we be there next evening?. . . (We had of course unfortunately to move on.) As they left, he shook hands with Sam, who had said that yes, he'd let his sister marry a black man. It is my own conviction that these men listened to us as they did, on the subject of peace, just because Robert Gore [a negro] was travelling with us. It made it more difficult for them to listen, of course; it made the talk more painful; but it also snatched it from the realm of the merely abstract. For the issue of war and peace remains fundamentally the issue of whether or not one is going to be willing to respect one's fellow man.'[3]

In this sense, the issue of nuclear weapons was intimately concerned with all these other, presently more current, political questions. They were all facets, as Goodman had seen, of one world-view. This was certainly the position of those organisations such as the Committee for Non-Violent Resistance and the American Friends Service Committee, who were just as concerned with desegregation and stopping the war as they had been with stopping the bomb.

But in another sense, too, they were leading the way forward, and this was in developing what might be termed the vocabulary of protest. For it was clear that part of the trouble with CND was not that it had run out of things to say – though these seemed less pressing now than they had before the Partial Test-Ban Treaty lulled people into a sense of security – so much as of effective ways to say them. Marches can only get bigger – and there comes a point when they will not get bigger. People get tired of doing the same thing, apparently ineffectively, year after year after year. But what else was there to do?

The extent to which new answers to this question were evolved in sixties and seventies America may be appreciated if we consider the phenomenal impact made by the Greenham Common women when the anti-nuclear movement was born again in Britain in the early eighties. The women very quickly became extremely famous, an international symbol of protest whose power was quite disproportionate to their numbers or situation. The extent of this power could be seen when the eventual installation of Cruise missiles at Greenham in 1983 was represented by the British Government as a stunning victory over CND in general and the fearsome women in particular. Yet, looked at in any logical way, there was no possible way in which the women could have stopped the British and American Governments carrying out their plans. Such power as they had was purely psychological.

The Greenham women's tactics consisted (and consist: they are still there) of several interwoven strands. One is organised non-violence. Another is the use of theatrical gesture, such as keening, web-weaving, symbolic break-throughs into the base, dancing on the missile silos. A third is that conflation of issues urged by Paul Goodman. In its first incarnation, CND had an active women's section, but this failed to make any especial mark upon the movement as a whole. By contrast, the notion of imposing a women's, not a man's view of the world – 'taking the toys away from the boys', refusing to see war or its implements, human or mechanical, as in any way glorious or praiseworthy – is a very important part of the peace movement as it exists in the 1980s.

None of these tactics or attitudes was familiar to the military or civilian authorities at Greenham, and nobody knew how to respond. A newspaper columnist dismissed the women as not being 'political in an identifiable way'.[4] Certainly their style was unlike anything that had ever made a mark on British politics before, and certainly they did not operate within the British political system. On the contrary, one of their firmest tenets was that the official political and legal system was completely irrelevant to the protest they were making. The questions it asked and demanded answers to were not the relevant questions. What they were questioning was the whole basis of the authority upheld by the system's assumptions.

But while this might have been new and nonplussing to those immersed in the British political and military system, it would have been quite familiar to anyone who had been in the United States during the Vietnam War, when the philosophy and power of the women's movement was growing along with the realisation of the mess the men were making of the world, and when the draft-resisters and their friends were working out their tactics.

In the summer of 1967 a group of hippies tried to exorcise the Pentagon. They raised two fingers at it in a 'magic' gesture and cried 'Out, demons! Out, demons!' They had hoped to encircle the building, but in this they failed. Members of the Mobilization committee who carried on negotiations for a permit reported that there were no circumstances in which the government would allow the Pentagon to be encircled by a picket line. Why not? There could hardly have been any danger to anyone in such a symbolic encirclement. 'Couldn't one almost say that it was the magic of encirclement that they feared – the affront to their authority that it would have meant?' wondered Barbara Deming. 'And so again the question: Were the actions of the hippies . . . as politically irrelevant as some feel?'[5]

It was a situation and question that would have been entirely familiar to the Greenham women (who have more than once 'embraced the base' by encircling it, and who frequently use the symbol of the witch as the female spirit) – as would the ensuing reaction of the authorities to this protest. In spite of the government permit for this demonstration, a number of arrests were made. The charges were all virtually identical – 'unseemly and disorderly conduct in refusing to leave a restricted area'. Yet the sentences varied greatly. Some of those charged were sentenced to thirty days, some to five or fifteen, and some were simply let go after coming before the commissioner. What could account for such enormous differences?

Partly this had to do with the temper of the commissioner – this, Deming concluded, made the difference between five days or fifteen. But more generally, the really important question was how you pleaded. 'If you pleaded not guilty, pleaded that you did not feel your actions to have been unseemly, you would draw the maximum sentence of thirty days. If you pleaded guilty or declined to contest the charge against you, the punishment was promptly reduced to a token few days. If you promised not to commit any such action again for a period of six months (some commissioners made it a year) and if you stood quietly while the commissioner delivered a parental lecture, advising you to "behave yourself" now – you could walk out of the door free.'[6]

It is a situation exactly comparable to that of those Greenham women who come up before local magistrates for breach of the peace and go to prison rather than agree to be bound over to 'keep the peace' – i.e. not to do those silly things again. What is at stake is what Carl Davidson of SDS – Students for a Democratic Society, another evocation of the sixties and seventies – called the 'desanctification of authority'. The contention of the Greenham women, as it was of the Pentagon hippies, is that it is the authorities, not they, who are at fault; the authorities, not they, who are criminals and ought to be arraigned. Clearly, if a great many people began to think and act in this way the power of the state to carry out the policy at issue would be seriously undermined (as indeed happened with the Vietnam War). In such a situation it is essential for the authorities that they reduce the protesters to the status of naughty children, who cannot be taken seriously but must promise never to do such a thing again – and essential to the protesters that they do not allow their actions to be so reduced. Symbolism is everything. It is the only way in which the state – in every other way so all-powerful – can be challenged by individuals on equal terms.

If the use of symbolism to challenge authority's legitimacy was one tactic worked out during the anti-Vietnam struggle, another was the use of non-violence.

The use of non-violent non-cooperation as a political tactic was first worked out by Mahatma Gandhi, and during his speech to the Court after he had finally forced the British to arrest him in 1922 he outlined its logic: 'In my humble opinion, Non-cooperation with evil is as much a duty as cooperation with good. But in the past, Non-cooperation has been deliberately expressed in violence to the evil-doer. I am endeavouring to show to my countrymen that violent Non-cooperation only multiplies evil and that as evil can only be sustained by violence, withdrawal of support of evil requires complete abstention from violence. Non-violence implies voluntary submission to the penalty for Non-cooperation with evil. I am here, therefore, to invite and submit cheerfully to the highest penalty that can be inflicted upon me for what in law is a deliberate crime and what appears to me to be the highest duty of a citizen.'[7]

Gandhi's example has been an inspiration to many, because of both its moral acceptability and its political effectiveness. In the United States in the 1960s and 1970s non-violence became an accepted method, part of the philosophy that sustained people through perilous times. It seemed universally applicable to the new view of the world that people were, in their different ways, trying to put forward. As Ralph Templin, a Southern Black, put it: 'We began under the inspiration of Gandhi, trying deliberately to bring nonviolence into the pacifist movement. But in studying Gandhi, it became a matter of amazement to many of us that there never was any real pacifist organisation in India. The whole picture was one of nonviolence used to end colonialism. . . There is violence in the very nature of the Southern social system, and nonviolence is being used to overthrow it. . . How can we say that our own use of nonviolence against a particular violence is more legitimate? There is a complex violence in the Western world. We have to think: where can we take hold?. . . We mustn't think that we can be against war and not against racism, or against the whole structure of colonialism.'[8]

Nonviolence is not easy to put into practice. One of its most interesting, paradoxical and disturbing aspects, as anyone who has tried this tactic knows, is the extreme violence of the reaction it tends to produce. When, in 1961, some members of the American peace movement demonstrated nonviolently at Electric Boat in New London, Connecticut, the makers of Polaris submarines, and were dumped, limp, outside the plant gates, 'onlookers would sometimes scream with fury: "Smack them down hard!" "Crack their heads on the sidewalk!" I remember' (writes Barbara Deming) 'one middle-aged woman in a light cotton house dress appealing with desperation to a nearby cop: "You ought to drown them all!" A young naval officer who wandered into the CNVA office one evening screamed at one of the women volunteers: "When the first Russian soldier rapes you, I hope you remember me!" '[9]

On other occasions, of course, the response has been less restrained. Anyone joining in an anti-Vietnam march could expect to be gassed and ridden down. Much worse things than that happened to Black civil rights demonstrators. The interesting question is – why? Why should non-violence – lack of aggression – evoke such especial fury?

What is the object of any demonstration? It is surely to draw attention to something the demonstrator wishes to question but which other people prefer to accept. Any demonstration about some vital topic such as nuclear weapons, civil rights, draft resistance, etc., is therefore a source of annoyance in itself. It is not only easier not to think about such things: often it is essential – the only way life as people know it, which is more or less as they want it, can go on. Thus, when the demonstrators at Electric Boat engaged the people who were abusing them in conversation, what finally emerged was deeply traumatic – the kind of fundamental contradiction, beyond reason, which if both entertained and disregarded will drive a person to despair. 'Most conversations followed a pattern. The man or woman objecting to unilateral disarmament would first declare that the country had nothing to fear if only it would keep itself strong, and not play the coward, "like you lousy pacifists." If we just kept strong, war could be prevented. The risk of war through some accident or miscalculation would be dismissed with a scoff. Didn't we think the people in charge were going to take such possibilities into account? But then at a certain point there would break from their lips some remark revealing the assumption at heart that disaster must come, of course, sooner or later; there was just nothing anyone could do about it. Many remarked that it was all in the Bible, after all. "Read Revelation." Many remarked "Sometimes I think it's what we deserve." Those who make this latter remark usually assume it to be daringly original. The uniformity of these responses is, in fact, striking.'[10] (Another example of such fundamental contradiction lies at the heart of the civil defence debate – of which more later.)

The demonstrator who is using non-violence as a tactic of course carries the complication and contradiction a stage further. The people witnessing the demonstration – including those trying to disperse it – are already having to face questions they would sooner not examine about fundamental issues about which they, too, feel strongly – for which, indeed, they are prepared to fight. But now the legitimacy of this response itself is questioned. Ought one to fight? They see the moral high ground – even this last, unchallengeable spur – entirely taken over by their opponents. No wonder they rage. (It is noticeable that almost all the intellectual rebuttals of the peace movement are concerned with this question of morals. Very few people these days pretend that nuclear war is winnable.) In fact, non-violence, making as it does its uncompromising point about physical aggression, is psychologically extremely aggressive. It is undoubtedly regrettable that it induces such fury, but it is small wonder that it does so.

It is hard to grasp these things, even – especially – in the heat of action. Here is the description of the arrest of a draft-resister: 'When the government came for Talmanson – "Tally" – his comrades sat in front of, behind, on top of the police car into which he had been put by federal marshals (limp and holding a volume of Lao Tse). Things stood still for about an hour, and then the police decided not to make the arrests that everybody had expected, but to beat people. Two people were sent to the hospital. This violence brought about a crisis of thought of those involved.

'The director of the church, Victor Jokel, shocked by the bloodshed, felt that the attempt at obstruction had been a mistake, and that only spiritual means of resistance should have been resorted to. Spokesmen for The Resistance declared that in the light of the police action they would have to review among themselves the whole question of nonviolence. Before this, they had been able to assume that if they remained nonviolent, the police would respond without violence, too. Now they could no longer make that assumption. "Nonviolent protest has two functions – to keep the participants from committing violence, and also to keep the whole situation from becoming violent. If the second function is lost, the first is far less meaningful."

'. . . Nonviolence is not a magic spell that one can cast over the antagonist – the psychological equivalent of the new paralyzing drugs. One of its functions is to minimize – in the long run – the violence an antagonist will feel justified in using; but it can hardly be expected to prevent retaliation altogether. . . If nonviolence as they have known it – that is, a relatively calm response to their nonviolence – is likely to become rare now, is it not precisely because they are beginning to challenge the war machine with much more vigor, beginning to show that they are capable of hampering it? To have violence come down upon one when one is not oneself violent is a very special shock. It is also the classic testing point for one trying this way.'[11]

10

Atoms for Peace

During the 1960s and 70s, the political front-line issues were civil rights and the Vietnam war. They were then the most immediate aspects of that holistic politics of peace advocated by Paul Goodman, and they developed its tactics and vocabulary. But although the issue of nuclear arms reverted largely to the back burner during these decades, that of nuclear power came increasingly under scrutiny.

1963 was one of those years which, in retrospect, can be seen to have marked a turning-point in political direction – certainly in so far as the public consciousness was concerned. The Partial Test-Ban Treaty of that summer marked a downturn in general concern about nuclear weapons. The same year saw the publication of two books which were to be enormously influential over the coming decade: Betty Friedan's *The Feminine Mystique*, the harbinger of the women's movement; and Rachel Carson's *Silent Spring*, which made people stop and think about the way twentieth-century man was destroying the planet on which he lived. Both these issues – feminism and concern for the environment – were to be of great importance in leading public concern back to the nuclear arms issue at the end of the 1970s. But during the early 1960s, they were naturally attractive to many of those who had been active in the fight against nuclear weapons but whose worries in that area were now temporarily allayed.

For many of those whose especial concern had been the way in which nuclear tests were poisoning the atmosphere, the transition to a more general apprehension of dangers to the environment as a whole seemed wholly logical. An indication of the direction people's thoughts were taking came from St Louis, Missouri. Washington University in St Louis, had for many years been a bastion of liberal thought in general and of concern about nuclear matters in particular. It was one of the few places happy to employ ex-Manhattan Project scientists who found themselves under a McCarthyite security cloud, such as Martin Kamen and Edward U. Condon. It was there that Linus Pauling had hatched what was to become his Scientists' Petition to the United Nations.

One of the ways in which this concern showed itself was in the publication, ten times a year, of a factsheet entitled *Nuclear Information*. This was put out by the Greater St Louis Citizens' Committee for Nuclear Information, and concerned itself chiefly with the environmental and health hazard effects of nuclear tests. It contained articles about such topics as civil defence and AEC underestimates of the health hazard to civilians. There was, for example, a controversy in December 1963 with Dr Gordon Dunning of the AEC over the risk the Nevada tests posed to young children in Nevada and Utah 'hotspots' – places receiving a particularly worrying level of radioactive fallout such as St George, Utah, in which there is today such an extremely high incidence of cancer that the inhabitants are suing the AEC. *Nuclear Information*'s view was the risk of thyroid cancer in infants was particularly high, as this damage can be caused by high exposure over quite a short period. The AEC view was that 'where measurements were not taken, the hazard did not exist': perhaps a fairly typical example of government reaction – any government – in situations of this sort.

This was the kind of worry which was alleviated by the Partial Test-Ban Treaty, with its ban on all atmospheric nuclear explosions. And after the Treaty was signed, it was fairly clear which was the way forward for this aspect of the anti-nuclear movement. Nuclear explosions were not, after all, the only aspect of modern civilisation inimical to the environment. In May 1964, *Nuclear Information* changed its name to *Scientist and Citizen* and announced that 'Scientific information about specific kinds of environmental contamination will now share these pages with articles arising from our undiminished interest in the peaceful and military uses of nuclear energy'. A member of the magazine's editorial committee was Dr Barry Commoner, the man who had encouraged Linus Pauling to

82

expand his address at Washington University into what became the Scientists' Petition. The environmental pollution issue was to make Commoner's name world-famous.

When the environmentalist movement first got under way, it did not particularly concentrate its fire upon the nuclear power industry, that inexhaustible source of safe, clean, cheap power ('energy too cheap to meter', as the slogan put it). On the contrary, people wanted to believe in nuclear power. Indeed, for many of the scientists, industrialists and public servants involved in the nuclear industry (and not only them but many others as well), belief in the benign nature of nuclear power generation was a deep psychological necessity. How else could they possibly maintain their faith, not only in their own work but in that whole notion of scientific progress towards a better world which had underlain the whole of scientific thinking since the seventeenth century? This necessity is nicely summarised in an exchange between President Truman and AEC chairman David Lilienthal which took place in 1949. Lilienthal had just given Truman the figures for the estimated nuclear stocks for the next two years. ' "This energy figure for 1 Jan, 1951, is really something," ' (wrote Lilienthal). 'His face was a picture and his eyes, enlarged by glasses, as bright as I have ever seen them. "Boy" he said, "we could blow a hole clean through the earth!" Then he said, "Wouldn't it be wonderful when 1 Jan, 1951 comes around, if we could take the whole business and dump it in the sea?" This gave me my chance to correct what I felt sure was a misapprehension, for I had found it in many places. "No," I said, "Mr President, that's the beautiful thing about it. All of this energy fabricated into weapons can be used without deterioration or loss for producing electricity and energy for many, many useful purposes, if only we can avoid war. . ." '[1]

If nuclear power was to fulfil the high hopes of its promoters, then there were certain attributes it had to possess. It had to be cheap to compete with fossil fuels. It already appeared to outperform them in other ways: it was clean, not producing the clouds of smoke associated with coal-fired power stations, and its energy potential, unlike that of the exhaustible fossil fuels, appeared to be limitless. And it must be quite clearly separate from anything to do with nuclear weapons including the possibility of explosion.

Even in the very early days, one or two people had had their doubts about these aspects of atomic power. In an article written soon after the dropping of the Hiroshima and Nagasaki bombs, although not published until 1947, the sociologist Abba P. Lerner wrote: 'That many people speak as if the danger of world war came from a revived Germany or Japan only shows what nonsense people will talk in order to keep away from the unpleasant "unthinkable" reality.

'A similar running away from the issue is shown in the vast exaggerations of the importance of nuclear fission for peaceful purposes and even in the concern lest extravagant military precautions should unduly interfere with the freedom of scientific enquiry. Scientific research is of great importance. The ultimate benefits from the utilisation of atomic energy for peaceful purposes may be tremendous. But surely every sane man would be delighted to sacrifice the next 10 or even 50 years of scientific progress if there were reason for believing that this would seriously help to prevent the next war so that there will be a world in which science can advance.'[2]

Not many such doubts were publicly voiced at that time – presumably because not many were felt. But by the mid-1950s it began to be clear that Lerner was not alone in his doubts about the safety of nuclear power. His worry had been that work on nuclear power would be used as a publicly acceptable mask for work on nuclear weapons. But the new worries were more directly concerned with the safety of the nuclear power installations themselves.

The point at issue was that of insurance. Anyone in Britain trying to insure their home or their personal liability against a nuclear accident will find that this is not possible. The reason given by the insurance industry for this blanket refusal is that such an accident is so unlikely to happen that it is not worth insuring against. This, of course, is financial nonsense. But the British nuclear power industry is part of the CEGB, a public utility financed by the government. Financial illogicality has been (as we shall see) an important aspect of its history, as has the ability and inclination of the government to draw a veil over things it did not want too closely examined.

This has not been true in the United States, where utilities are privately owned and must therefore be profitable and accountable to their shareholders. And by the mid-1950s the American nuclear power programme was already encountering insurance difficulties. It was not a question of the risk being so small that it was not worth considering – rather the opposite. In 1956 Hubert W. Yount, Vice-President of Liberty Mutual Insurance Company, told the Joint Congressional

Committee on Atomic Energy: 'The catastrophe hazard is apparently many times as great as anything previously known in industry and therefore poses a major challenge to insurance companies. . . We have heard of estimates of catastrophe potential under the worst possible circumstances running not merely into millions or tens of millions of dollars but into hundreds of millions of dollars. It is a reasonable question of public policy as to whether a hazard of this magnitude should be permitted if it actually exists.'[3]

By the 1970s, awareness of these potential dangers was no longer confined to the insurance industry. The general public, alerted by the environmentalists, was becoming alarmed – none more so than those members of it who owned shares or bonds in utilities which had invested or were proposing to invest in nuclear power. The Three Mile Island accident, which came within an ace of wiping out Pennsylvania in 1979, set the seal on their doubts.

The combination of environmental and financial disquiet has proved too much for the US civil nuclear industry. In 1984, a lawyer specialising in the jurisprudence of nuclear power stated that 'bond and shareholders are in the process of replacing anti-nuclear activists as the principal threat to nuclear power.'[4] Their alarm stemmed from the rocketing costs of the nuclear power industry. Part of these came from unforeseen contingencies – commenting on the costs of keeping the undamaged reactor at Three Mile Island in starting condition (between $80 and $120 million a year) the Wall Street Journal remarked that 'the nuclear power industry is a business that can lose $2 million in half an hour'.[5] But even without emergencies, the costs of making reactors safe and then insuring them are now such that the nuclear power industry in the United States is virtually at a standstill. There have been no new reactor orders there since 1975, and 110 cancellations since then.[6]

In view of these facts, the extreme attachment of many European governments to their nuclear power programmes seems on the face of it anomalous. Of course some of the reasons for it are understandable enough. They may, like France or Italy, have few fossil fuel resources. They may, like Russia, have such resources but in the wrong place. They may, like Britain, have political reasons for wanting to limit the power of the coal industry. They may, like all these countries, have invested so much, not just psychologically but financially, in nuclear power research and development, that the thought of abandoning the investment is considered out of the question. Or there may be another reason, unacknowledged but as pressing as any of these. In recent years both the environmental and the anti-nuclear arms movements have become increasingly interested in the question: just how separate are the civil and military nuclear programmes?

The separation of 'atoms for peace' (to take President Eisenhower's phrase, from his 1956 address to the United Nations) from 'atoms for war' has always been extremely important, both to the public and to those more closely involved with nuclear matters. A number of national and international agreements underpin this separation. The American 'Atoms for Peace' programme initiated by Eisenhower ensures that all nuclear technology exported by the United States is used only for peaceful purposes. The 1968 Non-Proliferation Treaty (NPT) prohibits the transfer of nuclear weapons or weapons technology from existing nuclear weapons states to any state not possessing these weapons. Non-nuclear weapons states undertake in their turn to conclude safeguards agreements with the International Atomic Energy Agency to ensure that nuclear energy is not diverted from peaceful to weapons purposes. The Euratom agreement concluded between the six original members of the EEC supposedly prohibits the use of civilian nuclear facilities for military purposes. Although these agreements do not cover everything or everybody (a significant number of nations declined to be party to the NPT) they ensure that civilian and military nuclear power are generally perceived to be safely separated.

So nuclear power and nuclear weapons always appeared to be two distinct issues. Although campaigners like Amory Lovins pointed out the possible connection between the export of reactors for nuclear power and the proliferation of nuclear weapons, that was not the main concern of the anti-nuclear power protestors of the 1970s. They concentrated on environmental questions: radioactive pollution and the possibility of catastrophic accidents. But as time went on and the issue of nuclear weapons returned to the front of the public mind, it began to emerge that they were not as separate as all that. France had never made any bones about the connection between her civil and military nuclear programmes. It turned out that Sweden, the Mr Pure of the international community, had during the 1950s and 1960s been on the verge of manufacturing nuclear weapons using plutonium produced within the civil nuclear cycle, which had been secretly funded and shaped by the military (who were pressing for the weapons) through the Swedish Defence Research Institute (FOA). Even after the Swedish Parliament refused the military permission to start building bombs, a secret circle of the ruling Social Democrats allowed them to go on building the necessary infrastructure in case public opinion should change in favour of the weapons. The key man in all this was an FOA bomb scientist, Sigvard Eklund, who between 1961 and 1981 headed the International Atomic Energy Agency, the authority responsible for seeing that no civil plutonium is diverted for military use. Mr Eklund was reported as saying, 'I never saw any conflict in working for the Swedish nuclear weapon programme within the civil Atomic Energy Company.' He added that values were different at the time.[7]

One country where the most strenuous efforts were always made to keep the issues of nuclear power and nuclear weapons separate was Britain. Britain has extensive civil and military nuclear programmes; and although the first reactor to supply power to the National Grid, Calder Hall, is a military plutonium-producing reactor of which electricity is merely a useful by-product, the two programmes have always been made to appear rigidly separate.

But with the resurgence of CND and the peace movement in the early 1980s, some awkward questions began to be asked. In 1980 President Jimmy Carter, in the subsequently-notorious PD (Presidential Directive) 59, outlined a series of new weapons programmes for the United States. It was clear that the plutonium requirements for these new programmes could not possibly be met from existing sources. The Carter Administration therefore had a problem. It was faced with a contradiction between this shortfall and its non-proliferation policies, which had included a halt to commercial reprocessing in the United States.[8] Then in 1981 came news of a new technique – Laser Isotope Separation – by which reactor-grade plutonium, which contains a relatively small amount of the Pu 139 isotope needed for weapons, could be converted into weapons-grade plutonium, even though not of the most efficient kind.[9] Soon there were reports that the new Reagan administration was seeking to buy British plutonium produced by CEGB reactors. The Foreign Office denied that this was for weapons use. Any plutonium supplied, they said, would be used in the US experimental fast breeder reactor at Clinch River, Tennessee. They gave further assurances that none of the plutonium exported to the States, at any time, had ever been used for weapons.

The CEGB and those sections of the British government concerned with nuclear power were particularly nervous at this time because a full-scale public inquiry was scheduled into the possible siting of a new nuclear power station at Sizewell in Essex. The whole of Britain's future nuclear power programme hinged on the outcome of this inquiry, which was due to take place in 1983. Among the objectors was the revivified CND.

One of CND's chief witnesses was Dr Ross Hesketh. Hesketh had worked in the CEGB's research laboratories as a nuclear materials scientist for twenty-two years, and had been quite convinced that there was absolutely no connection between the civil power programme and the military. When some friends raised doubts about this, Hesketh began to look into the question. He was unconvinced by the Foreign Office's denial of any connection between the export of British plutonium to the States and America's increased weapons requirements; and the more he looked into the history of British nuclear power the clearer it seemed that the links between Britain's civil and military nuclear programmes had always been of the most intimate nature. The CEGB's response to the questions he raised was to sack him. The sacking took place in 1983, just before the general election which was to return the Thatcher government to a second term of power – a government one of whose firmest policies was a commitment to nuclear power and to a rapid expansion of Britain's civil nuclear capability. In 1983, Hesketh presented his evidence to the Sizewell inquiry.

There was no question about Britain's first two electricity-producing nuclear reactors, at Calder Hall and Chapelcross. They were never owned by the CEGB, but by the Atomic Energy Authority, and their principal function was to produce weapons-grade plutonium. Hesketh went on: 'In 1954, a year after the Calder Hall discussions, a Whitehall working party considered "whether there should be a civil nuclear power programme to complement that required for military plutonium production". The working party decided that there should be a civil nuclear power programme: two reactors in 1957, two more in 1959 and a further eight in the early 1960s.

'Odd as it may seem, the Electricity Supply Industry was not represented on the committee which drew up the first civil nuclear programme. The working party completed its report in October 1954, but the Head of the Supply Industry, Sir Walter Citrine, did not learn of the existence of the report (or perhaps of the existence of the working party, the official history is ambiguous at this point) until the following December. He did not receive a copy of the report until the following January, and the copy he did receive had the details of the military plutonium requirements excised from it. . .'

Hesketh pointed out that the working group estimated that the cost of nuclear electricity would be 50% greater than the cost of electricity from fossil-fired plant then being built. Nevertheless it was decided to proceed, an indication of strong political pressure. He went on:

'. . . The White Paper which was published in February 1955 has a sanitised text, but the diagram on its page 16 . . . has a principal axis which begins with "uranium ore" and ends with "pure plutonium metal". The diagram shows three by-products: electricity, fission products and depleted uranium.'[10] (This perhaps shows the limitations of the classical training prevalent in the British civil service. Civil servants are trained to understand words, but not flow-charts.)

In the late 1950s the British military were very keen to acquire the American 'Nautilus' nuclear-powered submarine; but under the provisions of the MacMahon Act, the export of such technology by the US was forbidden. Britain and the United States had been at loggerheads on this issue for many years now: the British wanting to achieve what Prime Minister Macmillan termed 'interdependence in defence matters'[11] and the Americans, pursuing their nuclear isolationism, resisting this. But now Britain would have something to barter; and the launch of Sputnik, which showed that the Russians now had the technology to produce intercontinental ballistic missiles, put a different complexion on world events. Sputnik went up on 4 October 1957, and on 18 October the British Prime Minister, Macmillan, was on his way to Washington to begin negotiations for what finally became the 1958 Mutual Defence Agreement.

In view of the later declarations by the CEGB, by Whitehall and by Ministers that civil plutonium exported to America by Britain had never been used for other than civil purposes, the various hearings which surrounded the MDA negotiations make interesting reading. It was taken for granted in Washington that any plutonium obtained from Britain would be used for weapons purposes. Lewis Strauss,

Chairman of the USAEC, made no bones about this: 'I think this should be said: that our primary interest in purchasing plutonium is for weapons since we have no fuel use, that is to say, no assured use as fuel in the present time.'[12] General Starbird testified: 'It is my personal feeling any plutonium we can lay our hands on in the longer range when it becomes significant can be used to definite military advantage.' The price agreed for the British plutonium was $30 a gram, a fact that caused some heartsearching amongst Senators, since plutonium intended for use as reactor fuel cost only $12 a gram. But Commissioner Strauss explained that, since Sputnik had increased nuclear weapons requirements for America's allies, 'the plutonium which they produce and sell to us could be used for making the very weapons they want.'[13]

One of the diplomatic advantages to America of concluding a deal of this sort with Britain was that its reactors were not part of either the 'Atoms for Peace' programme nor of the US–Euratom agreement. The legalistic advantages of this – and the fact that the spirit of both those agreements would be contradicted – did not go unnoticed in Washington. Representative Chet Holifield, questioning Commissioner Vance of the USAEC, asked: 'Does this or does it not change the President's atoms for peace program to an atoms for military purposes program?'

Commissioner Vance: 'No sir, I don't think so.'

Representative Holifield: 'I think it does... It is a diametric and absolute change.'

A little later, Vance explained the differing views of the State Department and the Defense Department regarding the agreement: 'I think the State Department takes a dim view of this situation, to be frank with you, but I don't think their idea of diplomatic relations should be controlling in a situation of this kind. As to the Defense Department, I think I may say to you that if you will call the Defense Department before you, ... you will find that they will specifically recommend, as they have to us, that if we can buy plutonium abroad as a byproduct of civilian reactors and make it available for military uses, we should do it...'

Senator Pastore: 'But the State Department feels differently about it.'

Commissioner Vance: '... The State Department feels that it is

90

important that we take a posture before the world that we are a peaceloving nation and that we should be consistent in that attitude and if we offer to purchase plutonium from foreign countries for unrestricted use – and that is to say for weapons purposes – that it cuts across that position that they would like to see us maintain.'[14]

A few months later, in June 1958, the Ministry of Defence announced the modification of 'civil nuclear power reactors' for the production of weapons-grade plutonium. Mr Arthur Palmer, the Opposition front-bench spokesman on Power, commented that '. . . it is not entirely respectable that the Ministry of Defence should have made that announcement. . . One could understand that, in pre-1914 Prussia, the Ministry of Defence there might make announcements on civil matters, but it is a curious thing to happen in the democratic and constitutional Britain of today.' He estimated that the additional cost of running CEGB nuclear power stations as producers of weapons-grade plutonium would be between twelve and fifteen million pounds per annum per station (1958 prices). He commented that it seemed that '. . . the country's need for military plutonium has increased enormously in the last two years . . . the potential defence needs of the country for plutonium have increased to a quite fantastic extent.' Sir Ian Horobin, Parliamentary Secretary to the Minister of Power, blandly and uninformatively replied that 'Many chemical and other materials are of vast military interest.' He saw no objection to '. . . a great industry being put into a position where it can help the defence effort.'

Mr Palmer: 'There is a vast difference. The chemical industry makes manufactured chemical products, but the Central Electricity Generating Board is a public utility, whose primary purpose is to make electricity.'

Sir Ian Horobin: 'I am sorry, but that just is not so. We cannot produce these reactors without making plutonium.'[15]

To which Ross Hesketh, whose Sizewell evidence included this exchange, comments: 'The last sentence of this quotation could be rephrased: – We cannot produce plutonium without making these reactors.'[16]

While the Sizewell inquiry was going on, David Lowry, a researcher whose special field of interest is the connection between civil and military nuclear power, went to interview Lord Hinton, who as

Christopher Hinton had been chairman of the CEGB at the time these 'modifications' were imposed. Hinton told Lowry that he had been 'profoundly unhappy' about this, as one of his statutory duties was to provide electricity to the national grid at the most economic price, and this nuclear power stations, even before the 'modifications', were clearly not doing. But this did not worry the Government: 'In fact they forced us to fulfil the programme they laid down.'[17] As to what was happening to the plutonium so produced, Hinton was in no doubt. 'Some plutonium from the used fuel could be used for the British atomic bomb programme, and the Americans also agreed to take some for military purposes.' As for a recent statement by the CEGB at the Sizewell inquiry that 'Plutonium produced by the Central Electricity Generating Board Reactors had never been used (for weapons) in the UK or elsewhere', Hinton commented: 'I don't know whether it is right they should get permission for a PWR at Sizewell, but what is important is that they shouldn't tell bloody lies in their evidence.'[18]

This interview took place in January 1983, just five months before Hinton's death. More than three years later, little pieces of information on this topic were still being painfully dredged from the CEGB. In March 1986, Walter Marshall, Chairman of the CEGB (and a past Chairman of the AEA, so exceptionally well versed in the past history of this subject), when asked on TV 'whether plutonium from CEGB reactors before 1969 had been used for military purposes' replied: 'I don't know what it was used for, but it has gone into military stockpile.' He added, 'The Government said that very openly. There is no secret about that.' In fact the Government had never said any such thing but had consistently denied it, although it had by now admitted the exchanges with America under the MDA.

11

Protest Resurfaces

The coelacanth-like re-emergence of the peace movement from the political depths took everyone by surprise. This re-emergence was mainly due to NATO's 1979 decision to site Cruise and Pershing II missiles in Europe. As nuclear weapons emerged from the comfortable obscurity of the seventies into the light of common day, and the hands of the clock on the cover of the *Bulletin of the Atomic Scientists* moved ominously nearer to midnight, when World War III could be expected to be upon us, people began to rediscover all the reasons why these weapons made them feel less, not more secure. But there was more to it than that. The campaign was certainly focussed on a single issue – in Europe, to stop the installation of the missiles, in America, to institute a freeze on the production and testing of new weapons on both sides. But it was clear that this was also a more general protest. People felt themselves disenfranchised in the sense that none of the existing political parties or options represented their point of view on this or a range of other issues with which it was increasingly associated, such as feminism or worries about the environment. The assumption of power by politicians of the Right – Margaret Thatcher, Ronald Reagan and Helmut Kohl – exacerbated their fears. (One irony of this perception was that the missiles had been agreed on at the Guadeloupe summit meeting of January 1979 between Jimmy Carter, Helmut Schmidt and James Callaghan – two social democrat premiers and a President very far from hard-line conservatism.)

Nowhere was this role of the peace movement as a focus for many discontents more apparent than in West Germany, whose anomalous political and military status ensures a high level of political consciousness and activity. And if the previous incarnation of the anti-nuclear movement, especially that part most concerned about pollution of the atmosphere, had merged imperceptibly with the environmentalist wave of the 1970s, the wheel now turned full circle. Environmental concerns were to lead, via the German Green Party, right back to the bomb.

Nuclear issues had always been particularly sensitive in Germany. The vexed question of whether the Wehrmacht should or should not have nuclear weapons brought 300,000 people out protesting into the streets in July 1958, and began the feud between Franz-Josef Strauss, the then Defence Minister, whose dream this was, and *Der Spiegel* magazine, which opposed it, a fight which culminated in the grotesque over-reaction of the '*Spiegel* affair' in 1962. When, in 1964, the establishment of the Multi-Lateral Force did put these weapons into the hands of the German army, 100,000 people demonstrated at Easter at a time when CND, which had never seen such numbers, was already in decline. But by the mid-seventies nuclear weapons had retreated into the background of political concern in Germany as elsewhere. *Détente* and the success of Willy Brandt's *Ostpolitik* allowed political initiative to concentrate elsewhere: in highly vocal and organised student protest, in the extreme renunciation of non-violence by some left-wing groups who turned to terrorism in an attempt to overthrow the *status quo*; and in the environmental movement's protests against nuclear power.

It is hardly unusual for large-scale planning decisions to arouse protest in small local communities whose environment they will spoil. But when the farmers in the wine-growing village of Wyhl in Baden-Württemberg tried to register in the normal way their objection to the siting of a nuclear power station nearby, they encountered an unexpected difficulty. The Minister-President of Baden-Württemberg, Hans Filbinger, and his Minister of Economics, Rudolf Eberle, were both on the boards of the companies which had been awarded the contracts to carry out the project. Their interests were therefore all in getting the work under way.

Disgusted at what they had found, and convinced that it was quite useless to protest through the prescribed channels, about 150 people decided to occupy the site of the power station. These were not social revolutionaries but ordinary local people, and they were shocked when police were used to evict them from the site, perceiving this as the use of force by the state to solve what was essentially a political problem. But soon they were no longer alone in their protest. Their action had aroused a great deal of publicity, and the protest was joined by student groups from nearby Freiburg, by groups from Alsace across the border where there had been considerable success in non-violent resistance to industrial projects, and by Evangelical priests also deeply committed to non-violence. Thus an unlikely political alliance was struck between country people concerned with the environment, largely conservative and middle-aged, and young left-wingers, with a backbone of religious support. This combination was to form the basis of the Green Movement.[1]

The Wyhl events took place in 1975, and they caught and expressed the preoccupations of the time far more accurately than did any of the major parties during the election campaign which took place in 1976. In that year, starts were planned to take place on nuclear power stations in locations all over Germany, and events showed that what had happened at Wyhl was very far from being merely a storm in a local teacup. At Brokdorf in Schleswig-Holstein thousands of people took part in protests that began in October 1976, and whose momentum was such that a court decision in December to stop work on that project failed to deflect further huge demonstrations already planned. In other locations there were other enormous protests. An immense campaign of self-education about the potential risks of nuclear power began among local groups throughout the country. In June 1973, a poll found that 40% of those questioned thought there was no danger in nuclear power, while 48% thought it entailed certain risks. By December 1976, only 19% thought it was safe, while 70% thought it was risky.[2] The protests mounted, amid increasing violence. Many of the protestors disapproved of the violence, but nevertheless they disregarded pleas by the authorities to stay away. One demonstration at Brokdorf was banned by the State government, but this did not deter 20,000 people from taking part. In mid-1977 tens of thousands of police from all over the country were detailed to control 40,000 demonstrators against a planned nuclear plant in Kalkar, Westphalia, and many people seriously believed they were witnessing the birth of the 'nuclear state' predicted by the best-selling author Robert Jungk – a state whose projects can only be implemented by using a huge security apparatus. Worries about this threat to freedom increased the protests. In March 1979, 100,000 people protested in Hannover against the planned reprocessing plant at Gorleben, and in October of that year 150,000 people took part in a protest rally in Bonn – the largest demonstration of this sort hitherto seen in the Federal Republic.[3]

Much of the drive for these environmentalist protests came from 'Citizens' Initatives', local political activity groups concerned with issues rather than parties. By 1980 it was estimated that about five million people were concerned with local and national environmentalist groups, many of whom felt that no one at any official level really represented their particular interests. In June 1978, 62% of people questioned in a survey felt that this was true of many people, among whom 31% included themselves.[4]

The emergence of 'Green lists' in 1977 local elections was an attempt to gain representation for this constituency. These lists needed to gain 5% of the vote in order to be represented, and were soon succeeding in this. The emergence of the Green Party at national level reflected this growing success. In 1980, the year the party was formed, it succeeded in gaining representation in Baden-Wuerttemberg but not in the federal elections. By 1982, Greens held the balance of power in Hessen and Hamburg, and in the 1983 federal elections they gained 5.6% of the vote and held 27 seats in the Federal Parliament.[5]

Environmental questions were far from being the only source of political unrest in the Federal Republic in the 1970s. The dramatic career of the Baader-Meinhof group, culminating in the mass suicide of the group's surviving members in Stammheim Prison in 1977, was one of its expressions. Less murderous were the products of the 'Sponti' student protest movement, which by 1979 had set up literally hundreds of alternative projects including an alternative daily paper, the 'Taz' (*Tageszeitung*).

All this activity reflected a somewhat fragmented restlessness. Amid it all, Helmut Schmidt's original 1977 speech in which he demanded some concrete expression of America's commitment to her European allies went virtually unnoticed, and so, at first, did the announcement in 1979 of NATO's 'dual-track' decision, in which the siting of the new missiles was to be linked to arms talks. But the activity which now began all over the Western Europe soon found a response in German fundamentalist, pacifist and internationalist groups, who in turn

96

naturally allied themselves with the Greens. In its turn the peace movement provided the focus which transformed the hitherto rather loosely linked protest groups, each expressing its own individual discontent, into a coherent whole centred upon the Green Party.

What this meant was that the German peace movement began with certain advantages. It had a much more coherent political base than that in many other countries: it had its own political party and its own established newspaper – which was important in that it made members of even the most far-flung small groups feel that they were in touch with national goings-on. What could it not go on to achieve?

Within a multi-party system such as obtains in Germany, the influence of any small party is dependent on a hung parliament. The ideal situation for the Greens would be one in which an SPD/FDP coalition depended upon them for a majority. In a situation such as that under Herr Kohl's premiership, where there is a large majority opposed to their point of view, all the Greens can do is express that point of view – which means that it does at least get an airing. The other less direct possibility is that an established party such as the SPD will be attracted to espouse Green viewpoints, in the hope of attracting the votes that go with them. But in this case voters would be taking the same chance as British CND takes with the Labour Party – that when it is elected to office it may renege on its promises.

The political situation facing the British peace movement is in many ways just the opposite of that in the Federal Republic. In Britain, too, there was a remarkable revival of the Campaign for Nuclear Disarmament. Its membership in 1978 stood at 3,000, but after the announcement of the proposed missile deployments it grew exponentially: 4,000 in 1979, 9,000 in 1980, 20,000 in 1981, 50,000 in 1982, 75,000 in 1983, 110,000 in 1984. It has now reached the point where its paid-up membership is greater than that of any British political party. But its political dilemma has not changed since the 1960s. It relies for its support on people of all political persuasions and none. Its great strength lies in this very broad base of support. This is truly nationwide: almost every small town and village up and down the country can boast a more or less active peace group. Its members may not belong to CND but they support its aims and turn out for its demonstrations. This may well be the only thing on which they do agree politically, and although it is often the issue about which they feel most strongly, by no means all CND supporters would vote for the

Labour Party. But there is little doubt that the only realistic hope of implementing CND's preferred policies is to get a sympathetic Labour Party elected to office – and elected with such a large majority that it will feel able to act. The Ecology Party also supports anti-nuclear policies, along the lines of the Greens, but given the way in which the British first-past-the-post voting system militates against small parties, it is unlikely to make any real impact. Certainly there is little likelihood that the Liberal/SDP Alliance, in the case of a hung Parliament, would take on a Green role: Dr David Owen and his fellow nuclear enthusiasts in the SDP have defeated the Liberals' CND faction in that particular battle.

The question is whether, even with a majority behind it, a Labour government committed to anti-nuclear policies would be allowed to act. There is no doubt that, even in those circumstances, it would not be easy. Just because the government changes, that does not mean that those people who oppose the new plans disappear, or that they are less in a position to affect what happens. The Labour Party pledged to cancel Trident, remove Cruise and abolish American nuclear bases. In the opinion of those who know the Ministry of Defence, the first case, that of Trident, would be relatively easy, since it is disliked by all the Services. Even so, there would be pressure to carry on with it, since the Thatcher government has seen to it that the cost of cancellation late in the 1980s, what with the combination of penalty clauses and what has already been paid, would be such that financial savings would be negligible. The case of Cruise would be harder, because of its implications for the Anglo-American alliance, not to speak of the other NATO countries which were with such difficulty persuaded to take their share of the missiles; and as for the bases, that would be very difficult indeed. It would be strenuously argued that the most that should be done should be to remove the actual American nuclear warheads – which could then be flown in again at a time of tension.[6] The temptation for a hard-pressed Labour prime minister to seize on the last of these options and assert that he had fulfilled his promises would be very great.

An instructive comparison is that of France. Alone in Europe, France and Britain possess their own nuclear weapons. There is no peace movement to speak of in France, and a very strong one in Britain. But this does not mean that the French are less worried about nuclear questions, or are more aggressive, than the British. An international poll in 1983 showed that 44% of French people were worried about threats of war – second only to the Italians (55%). The British and West Germans, with 31% and 28% respectively, were the least frightened. On the question of whether nuclear weapons should 'never' be used, even in response to a nuclear attack, while 47% of Italians (and 58% of Japanese) thought this, the figures were only 27% in France and even less, 24%, in Britain. The British, despite CND, were easily the most gung-ho on this count, 62% favouring nuclear retaliation to nuclear attack, compared with 52% of French, 42% of West Germans and 28% of Italians. As for unilateral nuclear disarmament, while this was favoured by 35% of Italians, 25% of Dutch and 23% of West Germans, the British and French, proud owners of indigenous bombs, were far the least enthusiastic: only 17% and 16% respectively in favour. And only 12% of British and 13% of the French were willing not to increase nuclear arms even if the USSR did.[7] Under these circumstances, the surprise is perhaps not that France has no anti-nuclear movement to speak of, but that Britain does have one. Nevertheless, when the Socialists under François Mitterrand were elected to power in 1981, it might reasonably have been expected that France would join, or even lead, the burgeoning anti-nuclear movement in Europe. Not only did this not happen: M. Mitterrand went out of his way to endorse President Reagan's hard anti-Russian line.

Various factors have been adduced to account for France's failure to join the rest of Western Europe in opposing the missiles. One was a report on the bomb commissioned and accepted by the French Communist Party (PCF) in 1977 which, with a token show of reluctance, accepted the fact of the French nuclear force as a *fait accompli* and then went on to show how it could underpin France's resolve not to be dictated to by anyone – the French bomb could be aimed not only eastward but westward too. (The fact that should this happen it would drop somewhere in mid-Atlantic was neither here nor there.) Georges Marchais, leader of the PCF, underlined his party's support of the national bomb: 'The French are the world leaders in the atomic industry,' he told *Der Spiegel*. 'That is why the Americans are doing everything to prevent their further development. I accuse the opponents of nuclear energy of being agents of American imperialism.'[8] President Mitterrand, meanwhile, was an old socialist-Atlanticist in much the same mould as Britain's Denis Healey.

It is open to question whether, even had the will been there, France could have done the unilateral thing and abandoned the *force de frappe*. Any government wishing to do this would face exactly the same problems as an incoming British Labour government – notably, a small, secretive permanent bureaucracy used to formulating defence policy and deeply opposed to the nuclear disarmament line.[9] Another question is why, under these circumstances, the Government's life was not made more uncomfortable by members of the press and public. This may be attributed partly to the *sens de l'état*, a deep desire to preserve the dignity and unity of the state – as strong in the socialist ministers as in their unco-operative subordinates, and which prevented them from exposing what was really going on to the press. The press, too, has its *sens de l'état*: with a few exceptions, such as *Le Canard Enchaîné*, it does not ask awkward questions. Véronique Neiertz, in charge of international relations for the French Socialist Party, explained in October 1981, how 'since coming to power, the Socialists have access to information they didn't have when they were in opposition and which confirms the existence of an imbalance of forces in the Western camp.'[10] No newspaper was so tactless as to actually try and find out what this information might be.

But the media could not get away with this bland acceptance – and would not want to – if the public, too, did not go along with it. Of course, this can partly be explained in a circular way. If you don't know there's anything to worry about, you don't worry. And if nobody tells you then, as we have seen, where nuclear matters are concerned, the temptation not to think about these things – and hence to avoid worry – is very great. Certainly French policy is to impose, not consult. 'If you want to drain the marsh, you don't ask the frogs,' as Rémy Carle of *Electricité de France* famously remarked in relation to the siting of nuclear power stations.

There are other reasons, too, why these particular frogs fail to protest: French political apathy since 1968 and the reassertion of Gaullism; national pride and the conviction that in that part of the world free from blocs France could and should be the leader – a kind of moral imperialism of which the national bomb is an essential part; allied to this, an inherent distrust of Germany and of anything that seems to be inspiring enthusiasm there; the control of the media, and hence of the terms of the debate, by the far right, not necessarily connected with any political party; the presence of the intensely anti-

Soviet intellectuals inspired by Solzhenitsyn on the centre-left of the political spectrum, close to the Socialist Party, rather than on the far right, as in America and Britain.

All these things are undoubtedly relevant. But one cannot help but feel that one of the strongest reasons for an emergence in force of the peace movement in Britain was the election of the Thatcher government in 1979 – a strongly militaristic and nationalistic administration deeply committed to guns before butter, the peace movement's perfect adversary. In that loathing of Thatcher and all her works which characterises virtually all those who do not support her, passion returned to British politics – a passion which had been notably absent during the years between 1964 and 1979 when Labour had come to seem the natural party of government.

Of course the actual Cruise missile installation made a natural focus for protest which was absent in France. But it is difficult to imagine that a Labour government under Jim Callaghan would have pursued a different policy. It was he who agreed to Cruise at Guadeloupe, and his open hatred of the anti-nuclear policy to which Labour was committed in 1983 was the final nail in the coffin of the Opposition, ensuring a second term for Thatcher. And Callaghan's was the administration that ordered Trident. Equally, it is hard to imagine quite such unequivocal support for the anti-nuclear movement under a Labour government – for what might one not be letting in if one rocked the boat too hard?

As far as the peace movement is concerned, undoubtedly the most interesting development on the British political scene is the Labour Party's unequivocal adoption of a non-nuclear defence policy. Not the least interesting aspect of this is how recently such a stance seemed quite out of the question because politically suicidal. 'No prospective political leadership of the country under our present party system is going to risk presenting itself to the electorate with such a policy,' wrote one committed peacenik as recently as 1980. The reasons he gave were that 'politics is about power, and government is about holding the monopoly of force within a given territory. If a government were to renounce the nuclear armaments which help to guarantee its power, it would lay itself open to all sorts of charges' including loss of negotiating clout and 'laying its territory open to attack and take over by another power'. Not only that: 'Psychologically, it may also be true that such individuals cannot prepare themselves simultaneously to capture and control power and then to abolish or reduce that power.'[11]

Clearly, then, much has changed in the past few years. Indeed, it was only three years after that that Labour first went to the country with a non-nuclear policy – which did indeed turn out, for a variety of reasons, to be politically suicidal. Not the least of those reasons was that the party was, as usual, deeply divided on this issue, and opponents were able to expose the divisions.

Labour was once again defeated in 1987. But it seems clear that, in a peculiarly inturned and narrow campaign, defence was not the contentious issue everyone thought it might be. And before there is another election the nuclear scene may be radically different. It seems possible that we may be then confronted with the spectacle of Mrs Thatcher clinging to her Eurobombs while all around her the Americans and Russians are withdrawing theirs – a scenario at once bizzare, tragic and richly ironic.

12

America and the Freeze

There are certain similarities between the anti-nuclear movements in Europe and that in the United States. Like the German Green Party, the US movement developed largely from environmental concerns, and specifically from a vehement opposition to nuclear power. The most important American anti-nuclear movement is the Freeze, the initiative calling for a halt, preferably bilateral, to nuclear weapons testing and production, which would at least stop the spiral of the arms race. One of the most influential groups supporting this is Friends of the Earth, a group established in 1969 to promote environmental policies. Other groups drawn into the 'fate of the earth' aspect of nuclear weapons include the Sierra Club, the National Audubon Society and the Natural Resources Defense Council. And as was true in Germany – and is true generally – those concerned with the countryside and the natural environment are not necessarily political radicals. Throughout the 1970s there was enormous popular feeling in America against nuclear power: 150,000 people demonstrated against it in Washington in 1978. But the connection with nuclear arms was not generally made – as we have seen, indeed, strenuous efforts were made to keep the two issues separate – and many of the environmental lobbyists were emphatically not the kind of people who would support radical anti-nuclear arms initatives. This means there is a constant tension between those who want to push for more radical policies and the more conservative elements in the movement. But it also means that the movement is much more broadly based than it might otherwise be.

One consequence for the new peace movement in America is that the tactics which were used to such dramatic and devastating effect during the sixties and early seventies are not necessarily the most relevant or effective today. The theatricality and symbolism, the developed use of non-violence in the face of violence, threw into stark relief the feelings of a generation. In Europe, as the extraordinarily powerful effect of the women's vigil at Greenham Common has shown, such tactics are still an essential part of the protesters' arsenal. In Europe they possess the novelty effect of a new sort of politics – a rejection of the conventional circus as simply not addressing the question, a reassertion of the relevance of feeling and emotion over sophistry – which largely arose from the American experience of the sixties and seventies, and which infuriates and baffles politicians at all levels in Britain now as its equivalents did in America then. But in America, by contrast, the peace movement has begun to use the methods of the established political lobbyists, such as direct mail shots and the creation of Political Action Committees (PACs). What can work for the gun lobby and the creationists can also work for the Freeze.

A single-issue campaign must set itself two targets. It must first of all build up a wide enough base of support, local or national, depending on the issue, to ensure that no politician can afford to ignore it but must know that enough votes hang on the issue to compel him or her to take a stand. It must then organise its support efficiently enough to ensure that politicians opposing the issue are thrown out, and those supporting it are elected. This the Freeze campaign has set out to do.

The first Freeze manifesto was published by Randall Forsberg in 1980. By 1982 the National Nuclear Freeze Clearinghouse in St Louis reckoned that its anti-nuclear organisers were active in 279 congressional districts, with between seventeen and twenty thousand unpaid volunteers. In 11 State legislatures, one or both houses had already endorsed the Freeze.[1] As far as media hype was concerned, the Freeze's high point was the spectacular rally in New York, in the summer of 1982, coinciding with the second UN Special Session on Disarmament, when one and a half million demonstrators descended upon the city. After that, the media lost interest and the movement was pronounced dead. In fact, it reached a peak of organisation, expenditure and political influence during the 1984 elections – when, however, despite the 'Ronald Reagan Syndrome' which anti-nuclear leaders saw as swelling their ranks and infusing their troops with heightened zeal, the President was resoundingly re-elected. Nevertheless, the 1984 election was the first time that the question of the nuclear arms race had become a major motivating factor for public involvement in grass-roots electoral activities. In spite of Reagan's personal victory, five of the seven new Senators elected in 1984 promised voters they would support a nuclear freeze, while most of the Representatives who had led the opposition to the Administration's arms buildup were returned to office.[2]

Such a level of success requires funding and organisation of a level to boggle European minds. CND may operate on a shoestring, and so did those early anti-nuclear Washington lobbyists the Atomic Scientists, but shoestrings are outmoded in the Washington of the 1980s. In an issue-oriented political system with enormous prizes at stake, the battle for hearts and minds on Capitol Hill represents capitalist competition at its most cut-throat. In the early 1960s, instructions on 'how to approach your Congressman' (always be specific; make your point before the vote, not after it's been lost; stress facts, not theory, etc.) were printed in the literature any self-respecting peacenik would be likely to acquire, along with reports of various Easter anti-nuclear walks, local projects, etc. Such details of local organisation remain extremely important. In December 1982, when Congress was voting on production funds for MX, SANE (one of the original anti-nuclear groups, still going strong and now affiliated to the Freeze movement), together with the United Church of Christ and several environmental organisations, put out phone calls to their organisers in congressional districts. These local contacts ensured that the office of each local Congressman received more than 500 calls a week about MX, and when the Congressman came home he was confronted by citizen delegations, questioned on his position *vis-à-vis* the Freeze, and accosted on the subject on his way to church. The MX appropriations were not approved by Congress.

This campaign was a success – but it is very difficult to maintain such pressure over a long period, especially when the immediate issue is one – unlike MX – which people do not perceive as hitting them directly in the pocket and affecting their environment. Furthermore the anti-nuclear lobby faces formidable opponents. These include not only the military and those people with the kind of emotional commitment to nuclear arms which leads them to see any attempt to get rid of them as KGB-inspired, but, more importantly, the huge military-industrial complex – those thousands of firms controlling hundreds of thousands of jobs all over the United States whose work depends, directly or indirectly, on armaments. Between 1960 and 1980, US military spending accounted for almost 8% of the US GNP.[3] (The relationship between defence spending and high employment is another question, to which we shall return.) And the Pentagon has seen to it that this huge expenditure is spread around every state in the Union, thus ensuring that no Senator or Congressman is without constituency pressures to maintain it.

Clearly no anti-nuclear group can call upon this kind of corporate clout. Their job must be to activate those hundreds of thousands of private persons without whose support nothing can be achieved. They must be made aware of the issue, got working and tapped for cash. How is this to be done?

One way used by the Freezers was to put Freeze resolutions on to the ballot. Enough signatures can get any resolution on to the ballot; the most famous recent example being Proposition 13, by which State income tax was dramatically reduced in California. Freeze ballot initiatives were outstandingly successful in Massachusetts in 1980, and a group of California Freezeniks decided to try and organize something similar for California in 1982.

To get a resolution on to the California ballot, 346,000 signatures are needed. Much of the initial finance for this effort came from a liberal millionaire called Harold Willens, who has loathed nuclear weapons ever since, as a marine intelligence officer, he was sent to Hiroshima and Nagasaki a few weeks after their destruction. Willens could put up some cash, but not enough. He contacted wealthy friends in the entertainment industry, and also set about getting endorsements from Nobel laureates and religious leaders. It was then decided to enter the direct mail war.

Direct mail is one of the principal ways used by both the right and the left to contact potential supporters. There are firms in Washington specialising in direct mail shots who tap master lists of five million names each, both in the liberal camp and on the far right. The Californians employed the liberal firm of Craver, Matthews and Smith, and their first test mailing of 100,000 was astonishingly successful. In a typical mail shot, a letter is drafted by a copywriter and signed by a famous sponsor. With the letter comes a coupon which the recipient is asked to sign and return, affirming support for whatever the cause may be and enclosing (it is hoped) between $10 and $25. In California, returns averaged 3.5% (as against a normal break-even point of 1.5%), with some lists yielding as much as 8%; contributions averaged $25. 'The returns,' as one commentator put it, 'suggested a goldmine virtually unparalleled in the history of modern political fund-raising.'[4] Within three months of the California signature-drive beginning, they had 500,000 names collected.

The Freeze campaign now began to take off in a big way. Freeze referenda were approved in 8 states and 27 counties and cities including Chicago, Philadelphia and Denver. Only in Arizona and in 2 counties of Arkansas and Colorado was the Freeze rejected. With the approach of the 1984 Presidential election various groups within it began to organise Political Action Committees to lobby in Washington and to mark down 'hit-lists' of Congressmen and Senators they would work to see defeated and others they would support. 'Up to now we've tried to change the politicians' minds,' said Bill Curry, director of Freeze Voter '84, one of the activist groups. 'Now we're going to change the politicians.'[5]

With the Reagan landslide, the fate of the movement for a nuclear Freeze seemed sealed. Inevitably it has lost heart in a big way. Yet there remains a glimmer of hope for it. A *New York Times* poll in 1982 showed 87% of the population supporting a freeze. It is hard to reconcile this statistic with Reagan's huge victory two years later, but clearly what the Freeze has not yet done is to bridge the gap between people's intellectual perceptions and their translation of these to the gut whence all action derives.

The Freeze was an absolutely brilliant concept in terms of American politics. To appeal to 87% of the population a concept must be simple and comprehensible. To appeal to a large enough proportion of the Senate and the House of Representatives it must be flexible enough to accommodate a wide band of the hawk-dove spectrum. The kind of bargaining that goes on can be illustrated in the person of Representative Albert Gore Jr. of Tennessee. Gore supports the Freeze, opposed money for chemical weapons and took the arms control activists' position on many votes. But when he contested the Tennessee Senate seat in 1984 peace groups felt they couldn't support him on account of his stand on MX: Gore helped lead the effort to approve MX construction funds in return for a White House agreement to revise its stance in arms reduction talks.[6] But the peace lobby was also worried that if it failed to back Gore in his Senate race, its access to him later would be limited, should he win.

Such horse-trading is the very stuff of American politics, and of course the very antithesis of party politics. Not for American politicians the dilemma frequently facing British MPs of reconciling personal inclination and constituents' pressure with the party line. Indeed, the Freeze movement was seriously worried at one time that the policy would be appropriated by the Kennedy camp (Senators Ted Kennedy and Mark Hatfield rushed out a ghosted Freeze book in the wake of Jonathan Schell's best-selling *The Fate of the Earth*) – as this would have removed it from more general acceptability: again, the antithesis of European politics where it is essential to implementation that a policy gets taken up by a political party.

Conversely, it is highly arguable whether a policy so tailor-made for US politics is at all suitable for Europe. The very qualities which make it possible that, even in Reagan's America, the Freeze may win through – its broadness, its openness to different interpretation (so that one person may see it as a starting-point while for another it is an extreme policy which may be adopted for expediency and then watered down), its almost apolitical nature – render it, from the European peace movements' point of view, highly unsatisfactory. It is certainly unenthusiastic about the kind of activities usual in the European peace movement. When nine Catholic activists spray-painted a Trident submarine with the words USS AUSCHWITZ and poured blood down the hatches, the co-chairperson of Southern Connecticut Freeze denounced them as vandals and said 'We want to dissociate ourselves from that as much as possible.'[7] Certainly such extreme activities threaten the broad lobby. But in Europe such a reaction would probably ensure, as the 'multilateralists' have so far ensured, that nothing would be done at all.

The conclusion seems to be that successful single-issue politics in America is about equivocation, and in Europe, about how to avoid it.

13

Triggerpoints

Given the constant stream of controversial nuclear activity it is interesting to ask why indignation peaks at certain times and then dies away. It is not, after all, as though circumstances change so very much. Nor, despite the obsessive secrecy which cloaks everything to do with nuclear power, civil or military, is it impossible or even difficult to find out what is going on. On the contrary, the information is there: its availability, considering the efforts made to keep everything under wraps, is often rather absurd. The official history of the British electricity industry, published in 1982, contained many facts that the Government and the CEGB were still flatly denying in 1984. The same is true of another instance where scandalous facts were being brought painfully to light twenty-two years after the event – the British A-bomb tests in the Australian desert, investigated by Mr Justice McClelland's Commission in 1984–85. The second of these tests sent a radioactive cloud rolling eastwards over populous New South Wales instead of southwards safely out to sea, and elicited a cable from Sir Robert Menzies to Sir Winston Churchill demanding 'What the hell is going on?' During the Commission's hearings in London in January 1985, Lord Penney, who had been directing the tests, admitted 'in hindsight' that this test had indeed been unsafe. But this was known at the time, and stated in a book by Leonard Bertin called *Atom Harvest* published in 1957 or 1958 (it is undated, but appears to have been written before the disastrous fire which took place at Windscale in 1957). Bertin was one of the press corps at the tests, which had suffered 'repeated postponement' due to 'troublesome low-level winds' according to Penney's technical secretary, Captain Pat Cooper. Bertin goes on to quote Cooper's briefing on the test in question: 'On the day of the explosion low-level winds were present, but at 10,000 ft there was a steady SSW wind which did not, however, prevent the activity being wafted later eastwards towards the coast of New South Wales. . .'[1]

The facts, then, are available for anyone who wishes to know them. But people prefer not to know this sort of fact – or if they do know it, to put it out of their mind. The striking thing about the anti-nuclear movement is the way in which people have known the facts – the essential facts – all the time. They surface; they are made much of; people are horrified; they die away; they resurface years later, and it is as if they had never been known. It isn't just that people don't want to know these things, they actively want to forget them. Thus, much of the terrifying detail presented by Jonathan Schell in his best-selling *The Fate of the Earth* in 1982 can be found in *Nuclear Disaster*, by Tom Stonier, published in 1964. Stonier even presages the nuclear winter findings which caused such a sensation twenty years later (predicting that the smoke and dust from a nuclear exchange would blot out the sun and cause a disastrous fall in temperature over the northern hemisphere during the months following). But although the facts did not change nor become any more shocking (though computer models added detail and lessened speculative error) over the eighteen years intervening between Stonier's book and Schell's, one had little influence, the other, for its moment at least, an enormous amount. Stonier caught a moment when people had decided to think about other things; Schell caught them when once again the facts of nuclear life occupied the centre of the stage.

What triggers off these periodic moments of public concern? To ask this sort of question is, of course, like asking publishers how they spot a best-seller (indeed, the two may be intimately connected!). But if we look at the three times when the anti-nuclear movement has surfaced most strongly – 1945–6, 1958–9, 1979 – then the common factor makes sense of the obsession with secrecy. For these were, of course, all moments when the fact of the nuclear arms race – the fact that whatever they might say about unthinkableness there must be people planning actually to use these weapons, or why would they be making so many of the damned things? – suddenly came into high profile.

110

Thus, the scientists' movement in 1945 was really set off when the first bombs exploded. Some of the older and more prescient had, of course, tried to prevent the actual use of the weapon, arguing strongly – as in the Franck report – for a demonstration in an uninhabited area. But when Senator Fulbright asked Robert Wilson, a committee member of the Association of Los Alamos Scientists, how many of the scientists had been involved in the ALAS discussions, which were about the international aspects of atomic energy and the repercussions of their work, Wilson replied: 'In the days before the bomb exploded, about 50. Afterwards, everyone. At the first organization meeting, there were 500–700 present; the usual weekly meetings had 400–500.'

In 1958, the year when CND was born, the triggering factors were really the Sandys Defence White Paper, putting all Britain's defence eggs in the nuclear basket, and the explosion of the British H-bomb. And in 1979 the factor was of course the decision to site Cruise and Pershing missiles in Europe, with the accompanying perceptions that Europe was the 'theatre' American politicians meant when they talked about a 'theatre nuclear war'.

These proofs or reminders that nuclear weapons are increasingly the small change of military planning, sticking up like black rocks amid a sea of bland reassurance, have led to the long-lasting surges of activity. The military, of course, are as aware of this as any. The stated aim of the exercises in which cruise missile convoys drive from Greenham Common around the countryside of southern England is to make people so familiar with them that they are no longer noticed and no longer arouse comment. The aim of those activists who track every such convoy is to make sure this does not happen. Wing Commander March of the Greenham airbase commented that the convoys had to travel with 'indecent haste' on account of the peace movement's activities, whereas 'under normal circumstances' this would not be necessary. The head of security intelligence, rejecting the suggestion that the Greenham airbase should be surrounded by a 10-ft high wall, said, 'So far as is possible we would like Greenham not to become so much like a prison camp that it resembled no other American Airforce base in this country.'[2]

Again, the anti-nuclear movement was much more active in Holland or Germany during the mid-seventies than in Britain or the United States because it focussed on the debate about the neutron bomb which – since it was intended for use on the frontiers of NATO and the Warsaw Pact – affected them. The big and lasting reactions have all been about long-term military policy.

Individual alarums or disasters also produce a reaction, but not a lasting one. During the Cuba crisis, when events so nearly, in President Kennedy's words, 'became unmanageable', not just CND but middle-of-the-road opinion was that – to quote the *Observer* newspaper's editorial during that week – 'The ultimate aim must be the denuclear-isation of the world.' And although this did not mean that Russia and America must abandon nuclear weapons – though they should abandon most of them – 'Britain must certainly do so.'[3] But this reaction was soon forgotten. By January 1963, Barbara Deming noted, 'Now that the particular crisis has passed, people throughout the country are speaking and writing as though we had at last, as Max Lerner puts it, "regained some . . . freedom of courage and action." Many are writing now as though events had gone that week just as one might coolly have predicted that they would go. . . Have we forgotten the substance of editorial after editorial during the course of that week, of official pronouncement after pronouncement? "Our hope must be that Khrushchev will be reasonable" – these words were spoken in breathless chorus across the country. . . Can one really presume to speak of the "freedom of action" of a nation which stakes all its hopes for the future – stakes the future itself – on the chance that its antagonist will prove reasonable and humane in a moment of extreme tension?'[4] But logic – as we shall see – is not a feature of the nuclear debate; and the greater the terror, the keener people are to pull down the veil of forgetfulness which alone enables them to carry on with their lives in a nuclear world. Something similar happened after the disaster at the Chernobyl power station. Those German and Dutch politicians who hoped that this might help them at the polls because of their anti-nuclear policies were disappointed: a month later, memories had begun to fade. In Britain, on the same day, nearly two months after the event, that British lamb was declared still too contaminated by the Ukrainian disaster to be allowed on sale, the British Secretary of State for Energy made a speech declaring that nuclear power was safe, clean, and the only road to a decent standard of living in the twenty-first century, and that it was opposed only by foolish romantics. 'We must think of the legacy we are leaving our children and grand-children,' he said. Nobody laughed.

The real difficulty for a movement such as the peace movement of course lies not in arousing but in maintaining interest. How, after the initial surge, is this to be done? How are people to be persuaded not to resume their normal posture of preferring not to think about these things?

From the outset, it has been assumed that education must be the key to increasing public support for the anti-nuclear position. Once people know what is likely to happen (the argument goes) how could they possibly not agree with us?

To this there is more than one answer. But the conclusion of forty years of educating people about the facts of nuclear war seems to be that it is easier to instil knowledge than to make people change their attitudes. In a study conducted in America in 1984 among college students, substantial changes in what the students knew and expected in the aftermath of a nuclear war were shown as compared with a similar group of students two years earlier. Less than 30% of them expected any help with food or medicines to be available 'after a nuclear attack in which 50% of the population died, as opposed to 60% in 1982. In 1982, 63% of high school students and 70% of college students said they wanted to be among the survivors; in 1984 the figures were 41% and 19% respectively. Only 27% believed that a nuclear war was winnable, as compared with 45% in 1982. But this increased knowledge, or pessimism, had not changed their political attitudes. No more of them were inclined to endorse a nuclear freeze; no fewer of them believed that nuclear weapons are an effective deterrent to war.'[5]

A recent survey of attitudes to nuclear war among Londoners came up with similar findings. Of those questioned, 42% thought a nuclear attack was likely within the next 20 years, and 16%, within the next 5 years. Almost all thought London would be a target in the case of war, and that no food, water, heat, light, medicines etc. would be available in the aftermath. Only 16% thought they would survive the six months following an attack and only 23% wanted to. Yet if nuclear war threatened within two weeks only 40% of Londoners under 35 would join a mass demonstration against it; only 30% would use direct methods of protest and 12%, violent methods. The percentages were, as one might expect, lower for older age groups. Bear in mind that this was in a situation where almost all expected to die and most hoped to do so. And even faced with the threat of imminent nuclear war, Conservatives were much less inclined to rock the boat than Socialists. In this situation 51% of Labour voters, but only 17% of Conservatives, would join a mass demo; 37% of Labour voters, but 9% of Tories, would take direct action; and only 3% of Conservatives, but 20% of Labour voters, would protest violently. People resolve this conflict by simply banishing these thoughts from their minds. 71% said they hardly ever thought about it – once or twice a year at most.[6]

How, in such a situation, are attitudes ever to be changed? There is quite a body of psychological work on this, including a famous study about cigarette-smoking and cancer.[7] In this study, each subject was exposed to a communication which 'fostered the conclusion that heavy smoking causes cancer and which recommended that everyone should avoid or cut down on cigarette smoking.' There were two versions of this communication: 'a 'high threat' and a 'low threat'. Both versions included a standard set of paragraphs about the dangers of smoking, which discussed the relationship between smoking and cancer, statements about the seriousness of the kinds of cancer produced by smoking, and reassurance to the effect that one can avoid the danger by cutting down on smoking. In addition, the 'high threat' version included seven further paragraphs, interspersed, which said nothing about smoking but elaborated on the statements about the seriousness of lung cancer, the pain, the suffering and the poor prognosis. The parallels with the kind of persuasion the peace movement gives about the perils of the nuclear arms race are evident.

The findings, which were in line with what earlier work had suggested, were that the mild threat appeals produced far more attitude change than the high threat version. The authors of the study put forward the general hypothesis that 'When a relatively high level of fear is induced by the warnings presented in a persuasive communication, the recipients will become motivated to develop psychological resistances to the communicator's arguments, conclusions and recommendations.' Once again, the relevance of this to the peace movement – whose arguments anyway take place in a highly emotionally charged atmosphere unconducive to restraint – is obvious.

Human psychology is perhaps consistent. But cultures vary, and what may be effective on one side of the Atlantic may not appeal at all on the other.

114

The two writers perhaps most closely identified with the recent surge in the peace movement are E. P. Thompson in Britain and Jonathan Schell in America. Schell's book *The Fate of the Earth* was published in 1982, the year when more than a million people converged on New York in support of the Freeze initiative. Thompson's various publications, especially *Writing by Candlelight* and *Protest and Survive*, are deeply associated with the revival of the British and European peace movements. No two writers could be more different in their approach: and maybe their very differences may tell us what arouses Europe and what America.

Thompson's writings are utterly political. He castigates cant, secrecy, humbug and inaction, makes it clear that there is – or could be – a political solution to the appalling state of the nation or the world today, and urges his readers not to be lulled by the official line but to get up and take that necessary action. He is a pamphleteer, brilliant and inflammatory, and his writings succeed: they do inflame. The bomb and all its surrounding secrecies and paranoias are seen as political artefacts, and what can be done politically can – so long as the world still exists – be undone politically. Advocating his policy of 'active neutrality' Thompson ends his essay on 'The Doomsday Consensus': 'In the "new generation" of nuclear weapons we might subdue for a while immediate and manifest risks while centralized authoritarian power (and its concomitant management of the mind) encroached further year by year, and we drifted towards some unpredictable and unplanned contingency, an ultimate detonation. In the policy of active neutrality we would take an immediate and conscious risk, which, if we survived, would engender a new generation of human possibilities.'[8] This policy of a separate nuclear-free European grouping outside both NATO and the Warsaw Pact is that advocated by European Nuclear Disarmament, the group with which Thompson is most closely associated. One may agree with this position or disagree with it, but it does offer a possible way forward and it does assume that whatever is to be done must and can be done by the exercise of political will within the present world, given its imperfections.

Nothing could be more different from Schell's book. This first describes what the effect of a nuclear war on earth would be (reduction to a 'Republic of insects and grass'), then proceeds to a philosophical discussion of life, death and ecology, and finally assesses the strategic and political choices open to us. Although *The Fate of the Earth* is necessarily largely about politics, and frequently mentions the word, it is not really a political book – that is to say, it does not discuss, except in the broadest generalities, the political future. Its tone, rather, is quasi-mystical. Nuclear weapons are seen as a sort of Lucifer, almost with a life of their own, which we may or may not choose to resist. 'These bombs were built as "weapons" for "war", but their significance greatly transcends war and all its causes and outcomes. They grew out of history, yet they threaten to end history. . .'[9] 'Death, having been augmented by human strength, has lost its appointed place in the natural order and become a counter-evolutionary force. . . The question now before the human species, therefore, is whether life or death will prevail on earth.'[10] The feel is almost religious, and the solution propounded to the dilemma requires a profound moral transformation: 'The goals of the political revolution are defined by those of the nuclear revolution. We must lay down our arms, relinquish sovereignty, and found a political system for the peaceful settlement of international disputes.'[11]

Such a situation is so far from realisation that it hardly demands action on the part of the reader. It is in a sense the counterpart to that fundamentalist fatalism which welcomes the idea of Armageddon as fulfilling the Biblical prophecy – a notion which has been heard upon the lips of President Reagan, and which, with its concomitant prophecy of 'the Rapture' in which the faithful will be lifted up bodily to heaven when Doomsday comes, is central to the theology of such preachers as the Reverend Jerry Falwell.

Schell's suggestions for the remaking of man and society have a particular appeal in a country with a tradition of utopianism. In America, traditionally, people disgusted with the way the world works have gone off to some remote corner and founded their own society. Or, if that is not an option, they may try and remake themselves through analysis. Why not apply the same approach to society?

C. Wright Mills, in his book *The Causes of World War Three*, gave one answer. 'If history is fate,' he wrote, 'then everybody – and hence nobody – is responsible for such events as war. Then the purpose of analysis is to do no more than reveal the mechanics of our fate. Then there can be no serious expectations of any strategy whereby human will or reason can stop the thrust towards World War Three.'[12]

Yet although Schell's approach clearly strikes many chords in

America, this was not – as Mills indicates – the whole of the American tradition. Towards the end of his book Mills says that '. . . leading intellectual circles in America as elsewhere have not provided true images of the elite as men in responsible command of unprecedented means of power. Instead, they have invented images of a scatter of reasonable men, overwhelmed by events and doing their best in a difficult situation. By its softening of the political will, the conservative mood of the intellectuals, out of which these images have arisen, enables men to accept public depravity without any private sense of outrage and to give up the central goal of Western humanism, so strongly felt in nineteenth-century American experience: the audacious control by reason of men's fate.'[13]

14

Secrets

One of the most telling arguments against nuclear power has been that it is inconsistent with democracy. Even where it is being used entirely for non-military purposes the potential dangers (of radioactive fuel being misappropriated, or terrorist attack on a nuclear power station) are such that draconian policing is essential. The UKAEA has its own police force.

Security does not only entail policemen. It also necessitates secrecy. Some of the dangers of excessive secrecy have already been examined. It precludes informed debate and may be used to stifle it. It may be used to secure an easy life for a government that does not want to be bothered with having to justify unpopular decisions. And it has cocooned everything to do with nuclear power from the very beginning.

The utter secrecy within which the Manhattan Project operated was not abated when the war ended. The military took this for granted. The fact that David Lilienthal, the AEC's first chairman, did not, was one of the main bones of contention between him and his opponents throughout his term of office. For Lilienthal, this arbitrary imposition of secrecy over an enormous area of science interfered with the way America ought to be run. On 16 January 1946, he wrote: 'The War Department, and really one man in the War Department, General Groves, has by the power of veto on the ground of "military security", really been determining and almost running foreign policy.'[1]

What were these 'secrets' of Groves's – how secret were or could

118

they be? 'If my hunch . . . that in the real sense there are no secrets (that is, nothing that is not known or knowable), would be supported by facts, then real progress would be made,' wrote Lilienthal four days later. 'For then it would be made clear that the basis of present policy-making is without foundation. For present policy and commitments are made on the Army-sponsored thesis that there are secrets. And since it is in the Army's hands (or, literally, Gen. Groves') to deny access to facts that would prove or disprove this vital thesis, there has been no way to examine the very foundation of our policies in the international field.

'An amazing situation. For Gen. Groves determines whether a fact can be divulged, to anyone, by anyone, on the basis that such facts involve our military security. And that power over the facts has prevented anyone knowing whether we are on the right track or not. Example: the Atomic Energy Committee of the Senate has been refused access to the facts they thought they needed. Example: dealings with other nations involving uranium materials are not known to the State Department.'[2]

Such secretiveness was anathema to Lilienthal, the liberal New Dealer. It was alien to the American way of government as he saw it. But it had always been part of that of Britain. British government – the permanent officials of the Civil Service advising a constantly changing bevy of ministers – is run as between old friends who will understand each other with the minimum of exposition. 'It's difficult for an outsider to appreciate how chummy things are in the Civil Service,' explained an Assistant Under-Secretary to an inquiring American academic. 'You've probably known each other for fifteen years – lots of informal contacts and socialising. You ring each other up and gossip about things. Not everyone agrees with this style of doing things, but most do. Formal discussion follows after informal chats.'[3] As for the opinions of anyone outside the charmed circle, they count for very little. Public opinion is dismissed as not being well-enough informed. In areas where the public are the consumers – as education, health, social security, – discussion of course cannot be avoided and, where there is a concerted outcry against a particular policy, some response may be unavoidable. But in areas such as defence, the public is not expected to concern itself.

The unavailability of information relating to British nuclear affairs, however, has been surprising even in British terms, and almost unbelievable in American ones. Members of Parliament have routinely been kept ignorant of nuclear decisions – a gap that has more than once been revealed when the same information has been demanded on both sides of the Atlantic. In May 1985, for example, the *Observer* revealed that 'Britain has secretly agreed to US plans to deploy in Europe new nuclear artillery shells of the "neutron-bomb" type, according to American officials, who claim that Ministers are deliberately concealing details from Parliament.' The report continued: 'In testimony to a Washington congressional subcommittee, Dr Richard Wagner, assistant to the Defense Secretary, Caspar Weinberger, was confronted with denials from British defence ministers that any proposals for "modernisation" had been made, let alone accepted.

'In Washington, Dr Wagner poured scorn on statements made to the House of Commons. . . [He] was asked about denials by junior minister Adam Butler who said: "No decisions have yet been made on replacement of the existing 155mm nuclear military rounds."

'Dr Wagner said he disagreed. . . The 1983 NATO meeting "did endorse modernisation of the short-range systems."

'He was then presented with a statement in Parliament by Defence Secretary Michael Heseltine, which implied that Britain's decision remained still to be made. Mr Heseltine had then said: "We shall have to discuss which of the remaining capabilities have to be modernised. This is obviously a dual decision."

'Dr Wagner's comment was: ". . . I am rather certain they have committed to modernisation of the short-range systems."

'The rest of his explanation has been deleted from the Congressional transcript on grounds of confidentiality. It resumes with Dr Wagner being asked: "Is it their desire not to be explicit for home consumption?" He replied laconically, "Probably."

'He was asked: "So we are left with some vague generalities which we interpret one way, and the local folks in Britain and Germany are to interpret another?"

'Dr Wagner replied that he expected something "more explicit" from the Allies at some point, but "I don't know whether we will see a public statement that is more explicit than what we have now." '

The article concluded: 'The Reagan administration has had difficulty getting funds to develop [the neutron-bomb shell]. Claims that the European allies want, and indeed need it, for their new generation of nuclear artillery, are helpful in the quest for cash.

'But in Britain, any admission that more tactical weapons are being deployed with a potentially aggressive nuclear war-fighting role, will attract the attention of the peace movement.

'The "modernisation" plans were agreed at Montebello in Canada in 1983, at a meeting where linked decisions to scrap some 2,000 obsolete tactical weapons in Europe were presented as a step towards disarmament by the West.'[4]

Nearly two years later, the British government was still insisting that no decision on this matter had yet been made, and the discrepancy between this posture and documents obtained under the American Freedom of Information Act, showing that Britain had agreed to deployment of the weapons in 1983, was once again making newspaper headlines.[5]

This policy of silence on nuclear matters has been pursued by Labour governments just as much as Conservative ones. During Attlee's term, an MP complained, 'When we ask questions about "the atomic bomb" it is as if one had asked about something indecent.'[6] During Harold Wilson's term of office, this lack of information extended even to members of the Cabinet. Barbara Castle records in her diaries a discussion with Solly Zuckerman, then the government's Chief Scientific Adviser. Zuckerman opined that 'Ministers were still being successfully insulated by their civil servants from influence from outside. Most Cabinet Ministers were ignorant of half what was going on.' More specifically, '. . . Solly continued, there was one Cabinet committee not even mentioned in the official list – the one dealing with nuclear policy. To his own knowledge a paper currently being circulated to this committee was advocating the direct opposite of the Party's policy and he was just off to discuss it with Harold. It was impossible for anyone outside the Ministry of Defence . . . to check whether the paper cuts in the defence programme were really being carried out. In fact, they weren't. If I wanted to test this I had only to ask how many scientists had been transferred from defence work – as we had been promised they would be, so as to enable civilian R and D to be intensified. (How I wish there were a Question Time in cabinet! I know if I raise it what a smoothly evasive answer I shall get.)'[7]

The project then under discussion by the secret committee was probably Chevaline and, far from being cut, the defence R and D budget was being hugely expanded to develop it. 1967, the date of this diary entry, was about the time when Soviet advances in ABM systems raised worries about the penetrating power of the newly bought Polaris system. What was to be done? The Cabinet considered buying Poseidon missiles and warheads from the United States, but blenched at the thought of the controversy that would follow a decision to upgrade Polaris, which was after all such a recent purchase. It was therefore decided secretly to build a new all-British warhead with greatly improved penetration capabilities: Chevaline. The project was actually started in 1972 and became operational in 1982. Nobody outside the inner Cabinet knew anything about the project until 1980, when it was announced to Parliament. By that time more than a billion pounds had been spent on it, carefully concealed among sundry expenditures. By then, of course, it was too late to do anything about it – everything had simply gone ahead, cloaked in the comfortable silence of the 1970s. All that Parliament could do was to issue a report criticising the management and accounting procedures of the Ministry of Defence.

The British system of government seems almost designed to facilitate this characteristic combination of apparent accountability and actual secrecy. But even in the United States, with its unrivalled tradition of freedom of speech and access to information, the nuclear state nibbles around the edges – in this case, of the First Amendment.

The First Amendment states that Congress may not pass any law limiting freedom of speech or the press. Morton Halperin, discussing this, points out that it was 'viewed by conservatives and liberals alike as one of the likely casualties of the atomic age. Conservatives argued that we could no longer tolerate the lack of discipline in keeping secrets which characterized American politics, and pushed successfully for the draconian secrecy provisions in the Atomic Energy Act.' (Edward U. Condon, asked at the time whether he thought a fine of $300,000 would deter atomic scientists from passing on classified information to fellow-scientists overseas, responded: 'Hell, no! Make it a million!') Liberals, Halperin continues, 'voiced despair about the possibility of effective public debate when the president could plunge us into total war in seconds.'[8]

The First Amendment seemed to survive, however; and in 1966 the Freedom of Information Act was passed, and in 1974 amended, giving unprecedented rights of access to government information concerning national security. This Act remains the envy of the world. Attempts to

122

enact similar legislation in Britain are desperately resisted by the civil service and by whichever politicians happen then to hold office. Comfortable secrecy (such as gave birth to Chevaline) would then be a thing of the past.

The US government, it may be imagined, is no keener than any other on having its skeletons free to be hauled out of its closets at any time. But there appeared to be little it could do to prevent this. The publication of the Pentagon Papers, the secret history of the Vietnam War, in the *New York Times* in 1972, appeared to embody everything the Government most abhorred and the public most relished about freedom of speech and access in the USA. And indeed the Government did object. It asked a district court trial judge to issue to the *Times* a legally binding order to stop publication of the Papers on penalty of prison for contempt of court.

Morton Halperin makes the point that, although this case is generally regarded as a victory for freedom of the press, because the Supreme Court eventually ruled that the Government had not met the standards of proof necessary to secure an injunction, the important point is that only one out of the string of judges in different courts who heard the case actually threw it out, telling the Government that 'the purpose of the First Amendment was precisely to take from the government the power to stop a citizen publishing that which he knew'.[9] So although the Government lost that particular case, the thin end of the wedge had been inserted into the First Amendment.

Since then, that wedge has been driven further and further in. First, Daniel Ellsberg, who (the Government believed) had given the Pentagon Papers to the *New York Times* underwent criminal prosecution under the espionage laws – the first time these laws had been used to prosecute anyone for actions intended to lead to publication of information in the press, rather than transfer of information to a foreign power. The Government lost again, but on account of its disgraceful behaviour, not on the merits of the case. Then, in 1973, the Government succeeded in forcing a former CIA employee, Victor Marchetti, to submit the manuscript of a forth-coming book to government officials for censorship. 'These three cases taken together,' notes Halperin, 'established the fundamental principle that, in the right circumstances, the courts would assist the government in enforcing its view of what needed to be kept secret in the name of national security. It would prevent publication, it would criminally punish those who sought to publish, and it would require former government officials to submit to censorship.' Since then, these restrictions have been upheld in a number of cases, making it clear that, in spite of the First Amendment, the President now has great power to prevent or inhibit publication of information relating to national security. The temptation to use these powers in a crisis, to prevent the possibility of informed opposition to the Administration line, would obviously be very great: the effect is that of an *ad hoc* introduction of an Official Secrets Act.

The advantages of secrecy from a government's point of view are obvious, and this is nowhere more true than in nuclear matters with their embarrassingly contentious history. Protest needs a target: if nothing leaks, then very little can be done, largely because nobody knows anything is happening. But such areas, like black holes, can generally be detected by surrounding disturbances – the great smokescreen of lies and prevarications thrown up around them. One such is civil defence.

It is not surprising that civil defence has been at the centre of so many arguments about nuclear war. A person's views on civil defence reveal his views not only about the winnability or survivability of nuclear war but about the relationship between government and public, the élite and the rest.

Anyone advocating it on any large scale – such as the late Herman Kahn – clearly assumes that nuclear war is survivable, therefore winnable, therefore fightable. Kahn dismissed the stance that civilisation will end if there is a nuclear war as idealistic, unrealistic and unthought-out. But the implications of his suggestions as to what must be done to prepare for it appalled his critics. 'If certain physicists and military planners had their way' (wrote Aldous Huxley) 'democracy, where it exists, would be replaced by a system of regimentation centred upon the bomb-shelter. The entire population would have to be systematically drilled in the ticklish operation of going underground at a moment's notice, systematically exercised in the art of living troglodytically under conditions resembling those in the hold of an eighteenth-century slave ship. The notion fills most of us with horror. But if we fail to break out of our nationalistic and militaristic culture, we may find ourselves compelled by the military consequences of our science and technology to descend into the steel and concrete dungeons of total and totalitarian civil defense.'[10]

Whether because of cost or sheer disbelief, no government has yet invested its financial or political capital in Kahn's system of dispersed underground industries. Indeed, at about the same time as he was preparing his monumental *On Thermonuclear War* (published in 1960), with its projections of the time needed for industrial and economic regeneration after varying megatonnages of devastation in the United States, the British Government, while preparing to base its defence almost entirely on nuclear weapons, expressed its views of the matter by abandoning any efforts in the direction of mass civil defence.

This posture was consistent with the then NATO nuclear strategy, MAD (Mutual Assured Destruction) whose fundamental assumption was that nuclear attack was suicidal. But NATO's strategy has changed. Super-accuracy led to 'counterforce', the notion of a pre-emptive attack on enemy missile silos, adopted by Robert Macnamara in 1962; while the introduction of 'tactical' nuclear weapons together with NATO's rejection of a 'no first use' stance lowers the threshold still further. Complete abandonment of civil defence is clearly inconsistent with these later, war-fighting strategies; and, sure enough, the civil defence posture has changed. Mrs Thatcher's Government, a strong believer in NATO nuclear strategy, is equally enthusiastic about civil defence. Everyone is supposed to know how to construct a home 'refuge room' out of doors and sandbags. Yet the facts of nuclear civil defence – which caused earlier governments to abandon the whole enterprise as hopeless – have not changed. It is not surprising, therefore, that civil defence has become one of the peace movement's prime targets, embodying as it does all the contradictions at the centre of nuclear war-fighting strategy.

The governments of the nuclear powers have taken piecemeal, unsatisfactory and secretive action on civil defence. Indeed, it is hard to imagine quite what a satisfactory decision would be. The example of Switzerland, which has systematically been building nuclear shelters for years and where all new buildings must be provided with them, is often quoted. But Swizerland is a small, rich country, and moreover, being a non-nuclear neutral, is unlikely to have to deal with direct hits. Larger, poorer and more vulnerable countries have a different scale of problem. They must tread a delicate tightrope, and this is especially true in the case of nuclear weapons powers operating a deterrent defence strategy. Deterrence, if it is to mean anything at all, requires at least the illusion to be created that you would fight a nuclear war. Therefore you must have civil defence – but not so much as to alarm the public nor (as happened in Britain with the ill-fated *Protect and Survive* booklet) so ludicrous that all credibility is lost.

If you assume that civil defence in nuclear war is possible, the two big problems are: who should be catered for? And what should be done about the rest?

As to the first, the answers have been predictable. Arrangements have been made for alternative seats of government so that, in the event (the theory goes) well-drilled teams of essential personnel will move underground and carry on with their job.

These arrangements have naturally proved easy meat for anti-nuclear protest. The disclosure of the Regional Seats of Government was a rallying-call for CND in the declining days of its first incarnation, though its impact was primarily theatrical. A large part of that particular coup's point was the discovery itself – the revelation of the secret: though its essentially undemocratic nature certainly gave it added force. And of course the Spies for Peace were absolutely right – secrecy is fundamental to the nuclear state, and a large part of the peace movement's job is the unveiling of secrets.

Action such as theirs catches the headlines and may even cause a political hiccup. But although one may disagree with the principle it is hardly unexpected that governments will make arrangements such as this. Far more contentious, and far more revealing, is the question of what (in theory) happens to the rest of us.

No government has yet constructed the alternative underground system the thought of which so appalled Aldous Huxley. Quite apart from the cost, they are restrained by the knowledge that, should anyone start such a project – and for such an enormous undertaking secrecy would be out of the question – it would be assumed they were preparing for war. And even if the construction went ahead without incident, if, in time of tension, the decision should be taken to move the population underground – again quite impossible to do secretly – then the assumption would be that an attack was due to be launched – with obvious consequences.

What, then, is government to do? Keep quiet about the whole thing and hope people don't ask? The trouble is, they will ask; and of course, if we are to be expected to accept the notions of 'tactical nuclear weapons' and 'theatre nuclear war' they must be encouraged to ask, since such notions are predicated upon the idea that nuclear war is fightable and that there will be survivors. But what are they to be told?

Some of the things they have been told are quite famous. There was T.K. Jones's advice to get a shovel, dig a hole and get inside. This would, of course, solve the grave-digging problem in the event of an attack. But Jones, Boeing's adviser on civil defence and a member of President Reagan's Team B, was no pioneer in the field of ludicrous and terrifying advice on do-it-yourself civil defence. An early hand-book put out by the British Home Office advised people to whitewash their windows and soak curtains in borax in the event of an attack. Women's Voluntary Service speakers advised housewives to construct a refuge room in the basement or under the stairs and added, 'The longest you will have to stay in a refuge room is 48 hours.' That was in 1959. More than twenty years later, the Home Office was still handing out instructions on how to construct a refuge room using doors (unscrewed during the four-minute warning period?) and bags of earth, and equipped with bucket, body-bags (in case) and toys for the kiddies. The estimated time during which one would need to stay inside this shelter had been revised upwards to two weeks.

It is not that the advice is in itself wrong, but that the whole exercise, when considered in conjunction with the cataclysm which it is supposed to be addressing, is bathetic to the point of being insulting. Who (most people might wonder) do they think we are? Dr Antoinette Pirie, an expert on fall-out and an early activist in CND, tried to find out. She had 'a local WVS high-up' to tea and reported: 'She swings to and fro, saying: (a) they were themselves taught one thing but were not allowed to teach it as it was too alarming. Their instructions come from the Home Office. They are not allowed to say anything about long-term radioactivity; (b) they are talking to simple uneducated people so they can save some of them so it's worthwhile.' The Atomic Scientists' Committee was so alarmed at the distortions and simpli-fications of the WVS lectures that they offered to arrange a series of lectures to be given to selected WVS speakers. The Women's Committee of CND set up a deputation to meet Lady Reading, chairman of the WVS, to discuss this offer. But Lady Reading declined to meet them.[11]

On the face of it this was surprising. Even if Lady Reading deeply disagreed with the deputation's politics, the fact remained that they were experts offering to help her improve her service. Surely she should have listened to them?

The answer to this question of course depends on what you consider to be the function of civil defence. If civil defence is about saving people's lives in wartime, then what is needed is unquestionably the most accurate possible information as to what is likely to happen. If, on the other hand, it is about reassuring people and raising their morale, this is not necessarily the case – indeed, the two may be almost incompatible. But if civil defence is to be given a high profile as part of a drive to reconcile the public to the possibility of nuclear war, then the government is faced with a dilemma. If it tells the truth, the punters are unlikely to be reassured. But if it delivers high-profile false re-assurance, then it is laying itself open to exposure. This has given rise to some bizarre situations.

The activities of the British Home Office are particularly revealing in this respect. Domestic Nuclear Shelters, a booklet put out by the Scientific Advisory Branch of the Home Office, contained, as well as shelter-building instructions, diagrams and tables setting out the effects of a 200 megaton attack on Britain. (This was the size of attack generally taken as the basis for civil defence exercises.) They concluded that 'Estimates suggest that around 5 per cent of the land area of the UK might suffer seriously from the effects of blast [in a nuclear attack]. We cannot, of course, know in advance where the bombs would fall, but about 80 per cent of the land area might suffer no blast effects at all.'

This was very reassuring – in the eyes of some, suspiciously so. Philip Steadman, a university lecturer, did some calculations of his own using the Home Office data (they did not publish details of their workings). Steadman published his findings in the *New Scientist* magazine. He concluded that 'On the basis of the calculations offered here, I would set the alternative statement that "60 per cent of the population of England live in areas which might suffer blast effects." This is not very reassuring at all.'[12] Somewhat surprisingly, there was no official reaction to the piece. The Home Office neither justified its figures nor admitted any errors. Presumably it was hoping that no one would notice. But Steadman later found out that the Home Office had sent a letter to a local Emergency Planning Officer (responsible for local civil defence organisation) saying that he had since visited the Home Office and admitted that he had made mistakes in his

128

calculations. This was a complete lie, since he had never visited the place in his life, and had certainly not admitted that he was mistaken. The Home Office continued to refuse to discuss the alternative calculations and to cling to their own version of the facts. More discrepancies were then noticed, this time between Home Office calculations of deaths and injuries resulting from varying levels of attack and those (much more pessimistic) of the Pentagon. When the British Medical Association wanted to organise their own inquiry into the effects of nuclear war – doctors obviously being deeply concerned about this – the government at first tried to discourage any such inquiry. Later, the Home Office and the Ministry of Defence refused to submit evidence except in camera; and when this was rejected, sent in the typescript of a paper already published, but with the calculations whited out.

The BMA was not impressed by this. It said in its report, 'There are discrepancies between the projections for blast, heat and radiation produced by the Home Office and Scientists against Nuclear Arms (SANA). . . We have examined the methods for calculating the projections used by SANA and the Working Party believes, on the evidence it has received, that the projections from SANA give a more realistic estimate. . .'[13] The Home Office Minister responsible for civil defence, in a radio interview, went on record as saying that he 'did not take issue with the methods of calculation used by the BMA.' The Home Office's only retreat was into paranoia. It sent out a letter to all Regional Scientific Advisers in which it accused the BMA – a highly respectable and conservative body – of irrational bias in favour of CND. 'The style of this presentation, and the arbitrary conclusions in favour of SANA figures where they were deemed by the Inquiry to conflict with Home Office figures, reflected a high degree of bias towards the CND case, and lack of cogent argument or analysis. The report, as released . . . must be regarded as strongly influenced by CND-type propaganda; it cannot be regarded as an objective scientific document,' it warned. Nevertheless, it announced that it was revising its assumptions of the number of casualties to be expected from blast, and when these were eventually published, they tallied in most respects with those of Steadman and his colleagues in Scientists Against Nuclear War – the body whose evidence the BMA preferred to the Home Office's. Civil defence policy has not been revised in the light of these new calculations. What has been revised is the assumption as to the levels of attack which might be expected. The policy now is to be vague about these, but to suggest (for no particular reason) that they may well be very light.

These petulant refusals to face the facts are stupid, somewhat macabre, and maladroit. It is not too difficult to find explanations for them on that level. People don't like having their mistakes pointed out in public. And if policy is to keep morale in the face of impending nuclear war as high as possible, then this has nothing to do with facts anyway. Propaganda is propaganda. But on a deeper level the implications are more worrying and much less rational. The imposition of nuclear policy increasingly entails not only the abandonment of logic but – implicitly or explicitly – of the right to dissent, even in countries with a long tradition of political tolerance.

In Holland, for example, a country famous for its freedom of thought, speech and behaviour, the powerful church-led peace movement is – apparently – accepted as an established part of the political scene. But appearances, it seems, are deceptive. In 1985 a radical anti-militarist group, 'Onkruit', broke into the Utrecht area office of the Dutch military counter-intelligence service and obtained a large number of secret files and documents, including a chart listing 178 members of 64 organisations together with photographs of individuals. These were classified as the 'internal enemy'. The groups ranged from radical action groups and squatters through to such respectable organisations as the Church and Peace Group and the Centre for Non-violent Resistance. Those photographed included Mient-Jan Faber of the InterChurch Peace Council (IKV) and Nico Schouter of Stop the Neutron Bomb. A memorandum was discovered stating that 'the highest command levels of the military are interested in the IKV' but ordering that no written records of investigations of IKV were to be kept.[14]

In Britain, too, many anti-nuclear campaigners find that they are under surveillance – their telephones tapped or cut off, their mail interfered with, visited by Special Branch men. All this is quite illegal, since CND is not a proscribed organisation, and everyone is in theory perfectly free to express anti-nuclear opinions.

Several of the people who have suffered in this way offered their explanations as to the motivation behind the harassment. Nick Humphrey, who gave a controversial television lecture about the bomb's apparent thrall over the world, heard a pounding on his door at five one morning and opened it to find three men outside, who announced themselves to be CID officers from Kensington and Chelsea police station come 'to check you over'. They must have picked the lock of the outside door to get in; having found nothing, they went away. The police station admitted they had had no warrant and said, 'You can make a formal complaint but we advise you not to.' Humphrey commented, 'They do it because that's what spies do. They've probably read a lot more James Bond novels than you and I have.'[15] Karen Lewton, a former member of the editorial board of *Sanity*, CND's monthly magazine, regularly has her mail delayed and opened. She posits, firstly, the knee-jerk 'anti-patriotic' response that is so easy to evoke, especially among the kind of people who would be likely to join the Special Branch, but dismisses this as 'only the superficialities of surveillance'.

Lewton also thinks there are other, deeper reasons for these excessive, irrational and illegal responses to the peace movement in its various guises. Civil liberties and freedom of speech are a threat to the essentially undemocratic and politically unjustifiable way in which decisions about nuclear weapons are taken. 'There may also be a tacit admission in high places that, if popular acquiescence in the possession of nuclear weapons finally breaks down, democracy and nuclear weapons will no longer remain compatible.'[16]

Certainly there are signs that such acquiescence is breaking down, in Britain at least. They may be detected not only in opinion polls – which, as we have seen, often record opinion that is not translated into action – but in such facts as that so many local authorities refused to cooperate with the annual government civil defence exercise in 1983 that the exercise had to be cancelled. Since then the Government has fought a losing battle trying to force reluctant local authorities to make approved civil defence provision. By July 1986, few of the 54 authorities covered by the enforcing regulations had put these into effect. These details relate to Britain; but their equivalents could be related of any European country (with the possible exception of France).

Increasingly, then, nuclear weapons (and nuclear power) may be seen as being imposed by enthusiasts upon an indifferent or hostile population. Karen Lewton poses the question, 'If people no longer wish to be defended by nuclear weapons, how can they be prevented from having their way? Only by making away with democracy.'[17]

This may indeed be true. But it begs the perhaps more interesting question, which is, what is it about nuclear weapons that binds people so strongly to them in the first place?

15

Why Do People Hate the Peace Movement?

When one considers the quite disproportionate emotions evoked by the peace movement one is driven to the conclusion that nuclear weapons hold people in some sort of special thrall. Quite simply, the movement is hated and feared by a great many people.

This hatred is seen at its most spectacular in those places where a military activity such as Cruise missile emplacement has attracted particularly high levels of protest. When the Molesworth 'Rainbow Village' peace camp was bulldozed in the middle of the night on 7 February 1985, 'local people celebrated' (reported the *Guardian*). 'Mr John Hunting, who farms the field next to the base, said: "It is bloody marvellous – it's the best thing that's happened in two years." [1] When CND held a demonstration at Molesworth that Easter, local fields were barricaded, houses shut up, and children peered out nervously from behind gates. Clearly what they were expecting was something less, or more, than human. A large banner read CND GO HOME (most of the demonstrators were British, many lived nearby). As for Greenham, the local householders can find nothing bad enough to say about the women peace campers. One woman was quoted as saying she 'loathed them because they used the public baths at Newbury and they washed their filthy clothes in the washing machines.' A man wouldn't let his children use the public swimming baths because the peace women used them. He said that when the women complained because pig's blood had been thrown over them in the night 'he couldn't feel much sympathy because they had thrown it over themselves.'[2] These are extreme reactions, but they reflect real gut panic.

This may be dismissed as mere dislike of outsiders, the same sort of reaction as is reserved for gypsies. But if outsiders are in question, why should the women, who live in the woods and try to preserve what is left of Greenham Common, arouse so much more loathing than the airbase, which is a genuine eyesore with its layers of razor-wire and concentration-camp towers surrounding its concrete runways and missile silos, and which is peopled by foreigners? A woman whose house looks across to the base complained that until the women came, 'this used to be such a beautiful spot.'[3] She found the peace women, with what they represent, much more intrusive and offensive than the base, with all *it* represents. Why should this be so? Why should people whose only aim is to do away as quickly as possible with weapons which are generally agreed to endanger the whole planet arouse so much dislike – and so much more dislike than those whose lives are devoted to keeping the things ready to shoot off?

The bad old days of McCarthyism and blacklists are long past. But it takes more than the death of a McCarthy to alter habits of thought so deeply ingrained. They have become a reflex, unrelated in even the most distant way to reality. Thus in 1982, President Reagan, following an abortive effort to prove that Women Strike for Peace and the Women's International League for Peace and Freedom were Soviet fronts, announced in Columbus, Ohio, that the nuclear freeze movement was 'a group of honest and sincere people' who were 'being manipulated by some who want the weakening of America.' On 11 November, he added, 'There is no question about foreign agents that were sent to help instigate and help create and keep such a movement going.' But when the House Select Committee on Intelligence published its report on presumed Soviet disinformation and penetration of the Freeze movement in December of that year, there turned out to be no evidence worth speaking of other than the fact that the US Communist Party had urged its members to get as many people as they could along to the big Freeze rally on 12 June. 'But,' comment Alexander Cockburn and James Ridgeway, 'there were two more serious consequences. First, the FBI, hard pressed to trace the hand of the KGB in the operations of the local Freeze committee in Columbus, Ohio, is developing the notion that you do not necessarily have to know what you are doing to incur charges of collusion. . . Secondly, the pressure of red-baiting had led many of the immensely respectable citizens leading, or more importantly funding, the Freeze movement to accept the witch-hunters' premises even while rejecting their specific charges. By indignantly producing proof that they are not agents of the Soviet Union they have conceded the propriety of the interrogation.'[4]

The 'communist' smear is of course a very easy one (and offers evidence of the continuing hypnotic power of Karl Marx over the hearts and minds of the capitalist world). But while it is possible to believe that American politicians – so far removed from Russia in every way, physically and culturally – may be convinced by what they are saying, it is hard to credit that this is true of many Europeans. It is not that most Europeans see a lot to admire or envy in the Soviet regime. On the other hand, to them Russia is not a far-off and unimaginable bogey but a more or less close neighbour, peopled by human beings. Some of the appalled reactions to a recent BBC television series about the lives of ordinary Russians, to the effect that this was propaganda, that the BBC was simply being used by the Kremlin, etc., shows how much some people have invested in the retention of the 'bogey' image. But despite this sort of kneejerk reaction it seems unlikely that many European governments seriously envisage the Russian hordes marching down the main street, held at bay only by Cruise while encouraged by the siren songs of Mient-Jan Faber of the IKV and the Greenham women. It is simply not a realistic picture.

Yet in the wake of the Reykjavik summit, when for the first time it seemed as if there might really be an agreement between the USA and the USSR to phase out nuclear weapons, a curious and interesting state of affairs was revealed – namely, that when it came to the point, people who had been agreeing for years that an ideal word would be safer without nuclear weapons were thrown into a panic by the prospect of their actual departure. The weeks following that abortive but so nearly productive summit saw frenzied activity on the part of the German, French and (particularly) the British Governments to make quite sure that never again would President Reagan give them such a nasty shock. Although all had previously protested that (along with the rest of the world) they would wish, in ideal circumtances, to be rid of the things, they now asserted their deep and undiminished reliance upon the deterrent and peace-preserving effects of European nukes. After hasty conferences, Mrs Thatcher rushed to Camp David to (as one headline put it) 'bring Reagan back to earth'[5] and make him realise that, with the best will in the world, nuclear weapons 'cannot be disinvented' – and the President should not behave as if they could. The performance was repeated when it seemed in early 1987 as though at the very least medium-range missiles – Cruise, Pershing and the SS20s – might be taken out of Europe: the 'zero option' offered by Mr Reagan earlier in his Presidency and now actually taken up by Mr Gorbachev. Visiting Moscow at the end of March that year, Mrs Thatcher made a point of reaffirming that in her view the peace of Europe would depend on the retention of nuclear weapons there 'for at least the next twenty years.'

Cynical observers put this down to her fears that, with an election looming, an American inclination to nuclear disarmament would hand votes to the Labour Party – whose policy this was – on a plate. Of course this may well be true. But it is possible that Atlanticist European worries on this front are fuelled as much by the American right as the European left. If European peace movements are generally hostile to NATO (and to the Warsaw Pact), so, in a different way, is the new American right. 'Since 1977 Americans have been more or less openly discussing the possibility that the Western Alliance may be doing the US more harm than good,' writes Angelo Codevilla in a pamphlet for the Institute of European Defence Studies, an offshoot of the far-right Heritage Foundation. 'Today, whenever American newspapers report some proposal for military preparedness or political action against the Soviet Union, they almost invariably add that "the Europeans" oppose it or are sure either to circumvent it or to water it down.'[6] Are the Europeans worth the effort? Seen from the perspective of the sunbelt, the question hardly needs answering. Concern with Europe is merely a bow to history: the interesting part of the world is the Far East (or Near West) with its cheap, unorganised labour and undeveloped markets. This strong feeling that Europe is expendable (given such graphic, if Freudian, expression by President Reagan in his talk of 'theatre nuclear war' confined to Europe) matched with the anti-Americanism which is an undoubted feature of European peace movements, is enough to send shudders down Atlanticist European spines.

Finally, there are perhaps deep-rooted psychological reasons why the anti-nuclear movement brings hatred upon itself. One of the roots of paranoia is supposed to be irreconcilable conflicts at a deep level. Yet

136

the whole argument about the military usefulness of nuclear weapons is strewn with such arguments, which concern the survival of the world as we know it and which cannot be settled until it is too late.

The essential point about the idea of the bomb as a deterrent is that there is simply no way of knowing whether it works, one way or the other. Clearly there are many people who find the 'deterrent' argument convincing and, to that extent, comforting. Others draw the simile of putting methane down a coalmine to discourage smoking and naked lights. This would undoubtedly work, but it does not make for a reassuring sense of safety. At some point the risk will be too great.

Those who genuinely believe in the deterrent have made up their minds: we need not ask why they dislike the peace movement. But for those who are undecided, constantly to be reminded of the fundamental contradictions of the nuclear world – and the aim of the peace movement is to keep these contradictions before them – is not conducive to that peace of mind which brings liking in its wake. For the contradictions are gigantic, and both do not bear thinking about and yet must be thought about. On the one hand games theorists blithely bandy 'megadeaths', and nuclear shelter salespersons enjoin buyers to pack a shotgun in order to repel the desperate survivors who will doubtless try to break their way in from the smoking desert outside. On the other, citizens are advised that they will be safe in their improvised 'refuge rooms' for the fortnight until they can go outside, and that nuclear winter isn't a respectable scientific theory and won't be as bad as all those eminent persons worldwide tell us it will. On the one hand the most experienced military men – Lord Mountbatten, Field Marshal Lord Carver, General Gert Bastian, Admiral Gayler – assure us that as military devices nuclear weapons are useless, since no one can win a battle in which all will be killed. On the other, governments reiterate that they are an essential part of the military arsenal. We must have more and more of them because the other side have more and more and we mustn't be left behind. They are an essential part of our defences. But we will never use them. The whole and only point of having them is that they are a bluff to keep the peace and will never be used.

Those who oppose the nuclear disarmers must either answer or live with these contradictions. But of course in practice neither course is possible. The only way is to ignore them. This is what governments, and that vast majority of citizens who prefer to believe that those in authority ultimately know best, try to do. The crime of the anti-nuclear movement is that it tries to do just the opposite: it points out these intolerable contradictions as loudly and insistently as it can. As Sir Frank Cooper, ex-head of the British Ministry of Defence, put it, 'The greatest disservice CND has done is to mouth platitudes.' Unfortunately they are not platitudes with which it is possible to live. But people do not like to be reminded of these things. If they cannot, like the ancient Greeks, kill the bearer of bad news, they can and do hate him.

16

Religious War and Religious Peace

In March 1960, midway between the Labour Party conference which came out against nuclear weapons and that in which Hugh Gaitskell got this position reversed, Richard Crossman records an exchange between himself and Gaitskell. Discussing Gaitskell's preference for reliance on nuclear weapons rather than conscription and a large conventional army, Crossman said, 'You may be right that the Party as such was bound to condone this wicked –

GAITSKELL: I wish you wouldn't use words like wicked. They're so emotional and extreme!'[1]

It is true that emotional extremism and practical politics should if possible be separated. Unfortunately this is difficult in the case of nuclear weapons – one of the central political issues of our time. This is hardly surprising, since the kind of prospects under discussion – the killing of millions by a bolt from the blue, the end of our civilisation, the transformation of the western hemisphere into a radioactive desert – are beyond the rational imagination. Any attempt to corral them into acceptably political terms results in the crazy, distanced world of the strategic studies gamesplayers, with their talk of 'countervalue devastation' and 'environmental counterforce'. Only religious terminology can express these things satisfactorily – even the arch-rationalist Herman Kahn posited a 'Doomsday machine'. And it is an historical cliché that Robert Oppenheimer, witnessing the first atomic explosion at Alamogordo, called to mind lines from the Hindu sacred text, the *Bhagavadgita*: 'If the radiance of a thousand suns were to

burst into the sky that would be like the splendour of the Mighty One'
— while the mushroom cloud rising afterwards evoked another line
from the same source: 'I am become Death, the shatterer of worlds.'

It is hardly surprising, then, that religion and the bomb have become
inextricably intertwined. Politics is *ipso facto* mundane; but
mundanities can only diminish the realities of nuclear weapons. That,
of course, is why politicians and others who are committed to nuclear
weapons prefer to retrict their discussion to such terms, reducing
religion, in this instance, to the level of politics. Richard Perle,
Reagan's arch-hawk, dismissed the European peace movements, in a
memorable phrase, as 'Protestant angst'. According to Perle, the
churches in northern Europe, distressed at declining membership,
seized on the nuclear issue to bring in young people and revive flagging
attendances. 'If the way to bring young people into the church is to
have seminars on GLCMs [Cruise missiles] and Pershing IIs, you can
hardly blame the clergy for holding seminars on GLCMs and Pershing
IIs.'[2]

But which came first, the chicken or the egg? Various British church
leaders have said quite openly that the nuclear disarmament
movement offers immense opportunities for the churches to reach new
audiences and show their relevance to vital issues of the modern
world. Conversely, 'if Christians refuse to join with those who make a
peaceful protest against preparation for mass murder, then can you
blame CND followers if they excise Christianity from their lives for
good?'[3]

However, rather than a weak church gaining strength and authority
on the back of the anti-nuclear movement — as religious leaders hoped
might happen in Britain — it has, in the countries where it was already
strong, been the backbone of that movement. In Holland, the
Interchurch Peace Council, IKV, founded in 1966, launched a
longterm campaign in 1977 around the slogan: 'Help rid the world of
nuclear weapons. Let it begin in the Netherlands.' What first exercised
the Dutch movement was the neutron bomb, apparently destined to be
deployed in Holland, but after 1979 concern centred on Cruise
deployment. So strong was the movement that the Dutch Parliament
actually voted against Cruise; this was softened to a delay, after which,
if various conditions were not met, Cruise would be, and in 1985
finally was, deployed.

One political advantage of church leadership in the western peace

140

movement is that the facile 'KGB front' gibe can hardly be made to stick. (This, and the implied association with undesirable leftists, is one reason why Anglican traditionalists, 'the Tory party at prayer', were so incensed with the report of the Church of England working party on this subject, *The Church and the Bomb*, which recommended taking 'unilateral measures at the start in the hope of getting multilateral reductions moving.'[4]) Certainly Moscow distrusts Church-based movements; the Dutch Christian Democrat Prime Minister, Ruud Lubbers, was able to capitalise on this by making one of the hypothetical conditions under which Holland would reject Cruise a Russian freeze on SS20 deployment. He thus hoped to turn the anti-missile protests of Moscow's least-favourite peace movement (the Russians disliked the IKV's emphasis on 'detente from below') against Moscow rather than Washington.

The IKV includes both Protestants and Catholics. But in Germany it is the Protestant Church which has been a centre for political protest. In West Germany this dates largely from 1981, when the synod of the Evangelical Church in Hamburg drew 150,000 participants. The official theme was 'Fear Not'; the youth imposed on this their own theme – 'Have Fear: Atomic Death Threatens Us All.' The Church's endorsement of the peace movement won its respect among the young people: the Evangelical Congress in Hanover, in June 1983, attracted 200,000, mostly young people. In the Federal Republic, the young protesters are in revolt against the whole value-system of their elders, and the peace movement is merely one expression of an alternative culture that rejects social organisations of both left and right. The Church, standing outside the political system and the whole *'system-konform'* materialist world, is an acceptable centre for protest.

In East Germany the involvement of the Church with the peace movement has come about somewhat differently. The relaxation of the *'Ostpolitik'* years saw a partial reconciliation between the state and the powerful Evangelical Church. The Church is opposed to militarism, and after the reintroduction of conscription in the 1950s, pressured the state party, the SED, into introducing a special construction division of army service without weapons for religious objectors. When, in 1978, military education was made compulsory in the ninth and tenth grades of school, the Church supported anxious parents in objecting to this and the attitudes to 'the enemy' that it would give rise to; a number of 'peace education' initiatives arose at

141

parish and church level. This was, of course, the time of the resurgence of the anti-nuclear movement in the NATO countries, and while the SED accorded this maximum publicity, it was not enthusiastic at the prospect of comparable mobilisations at home. It (like all the Warsaw Pact countries) introduced its own 'official' peace movement, with such slogans as 'Make Peace Against NATO' and 'Peace Must Be Defended, Peace Must Be Armed'. It was natural for the unofficial movement to centre itself upon the Church, the anti-militaristic and officially countenanced opposition to these aspects of the state.

The make-up of the Church-based peace movement in the East is, however, rather different from that of the equivalent West German movement, which consists largely – as does the peace movement elsewhere in the West – of the educated middle class. In the GDR, however, it is made up not of those who are able to get into university and might jeopardize professional careers, but mainly of young manual workers and apprentices like the one who explained, 'I am only 19, and already I have nothing more to lose.'[5]

Clearly the Church can only play this kind of central role in a mass movement where it plays an equally central role in the life of the people. Thus, although various churches play an important role in the British peace movement, they are not central to it because they are not central to the life of most Britons. The same is increasingly true of the European Catholic countries, where, in any case, progressive politics and a conservative Church have generally been at daggers drawn.

What, though, of America? The United States is perhaps the most religious country in the Western world today. On any single Sunday, almost as many Americans attend church as go to all the major sporting events held in the United States during an entire year.[6]

Religious groups have traditionally been both active and effective in American politics, most notably in the campaigns for the abolition of slavery, for Prohibition, civil rights and withdrawal from Vietnam. With the exception of Prohibition, which can hardly be so categorised, these interventions have been on the radical side and have been led by nonconformist groups, notably the Quakers, whose Friends Service Committee is almost always in the vanguard of the action. The peace movement has been no exception in this respect. A young woman Presbyterian minister, Jan Orr-Harter, has been one of the mainstays of the Freeze national committee since its inception in 1980. The Freeze's endorsement by the Presbyterians spread rapidly to other

142

denominations; when it mushroomed in 1982, a *Washington Post* reporter telephoned her to ask for an explanation. ' "Jesus," she replied. "He was so flabbergasted he hung up the phone and printed it." '[7] The radical Catholic Daniel Berrigan was one of the group calling themselves the Plowshares 8 whose action in penetrating the Trident dockyard and hitting one of the missiles on the nosecone with a hammer outraged Middle America: 'This time you have gone too far,' spluttered the judge, sentencing them to a year's imprisonment. A group calling itself the Agape Community monitors the infamous White Train which moves nuclear warheads to their destinations after their assembly at the Pantex factory in Amarillo, Texas.

Such involvement may be admirable (or not, according to your views) but it is hardly extraordinary. Religious activists have often taken such stands. But some peculiar things have been happening on the religious front in America during the past few years. The religious left and right are engaged in a battle, and some unexpected positions are being taken up.

Perhaps the greatest and least anticipated fillip to the anti-nuclear stance came with the Pastoral Letter of the Roman Catholic Bishops, 'The Challenge of Peace', drafted painfully over several years and finally published and distributed to all congregations in 1983. Of all the possible directions from which support for the anti-nuclear movement might come, this must have been about the least expected. The Roman Catholic Church is noted for its conservatism. On nuclear matters it first expressed itself through Pope Pius XII in the 1950s, who argued that the nuclear threat was only quantitively, not qualitatively new, and declared that 'a Catholic cannot invoke his own conscience in order to refuse to serve and fulfill those duties that the law imposes' in matters related to the state and defence.[8] It was clear that in the minds of the Pope and of many prominent Catholics, war against Russia could be considered a 'just war' – a concept which has featured in theological discussions since medieval times and which is now once again a matter of some controversy.

The war uppermost in people's minds at that time was the one in Korea, in which General Douglas MacArthur had, in the late summer of 1950, done his best to launch a preventive crusade against communism in China, to the horror of President Truman. In the midst of this controversy, while Truman was trying to pass off MacArthur's raids over the Chinese border as 'mistakes', the Secretary of the Navy,

143

Francis P. Matthews, a prominent Catholic layman, made a speech in Boston advocating preventive war and declaring this would 'cast us in a character new to a true democracy – an initiator of a war of aggression . . . the first aggressors for peace.' This bizarre logic was eagerly welcomed by some of the military: a few days later Major General Orvil A. Anderson was suspended as Commandant of the Air War College for having taught a course of lectures on 'preventive war strategy' and for an interview in which he advocated an attack on Russia, saying, 'Give me the order to do it and I can break up Russia's five A-bomb nests in a week. . . And when I went up to Christ – I think I could explain to him that I had saved civilisation.'[9] (The prevailing hysterical and paranoid concept of patriotism can be judged from the one dissenting opinion in the Oppenheimer case in 1954. Professor Ward Evans thought there was not 'the slightest vestige of information' to suggest that Oppenheimer was not loyal and added '– as if this was the highest recommendation – "He hates Russia." '[10]

The Vatican's position has, of course, moved on since then. The 1963 Papal Encyclical '*Pacem in Terris*' asserts that nuclear issues are in fact new to mankind; and when Pope John Paul II visited Hiroshima in 1981 he remarked that everyone must now face 'a basic moral consideration: from now on, it is only through a conscious choice and then deliberate policy that humanity can survive.'[11]

These comments were gratefully seized upon by that large number of Catholic clergy who support Pax Christi, the Catholic peace organisation. These include 60 members of the American Catholic hierarchy (among them Bishop Leroy Matthiesen of Amarillo, whose diocese includes the Pantex plant). The influence of Matthiesen and other Pax Christi bishops ensured that the pacifist passages in the Pastoral Letter were strengthened. The Letter rejects outright pacifism in favour of 'just war' properly understood – but with considerable uncertainty over whether nuclear war can be squeezed into any such criteria. For instance, 'Under no circumstances may nuclear weapons or other instruments of mass slaughter be used for the purpose of destroying population centers or other predominantly civilian targets' – a difficult one for nuclear strategists: what if military targets are located in or near population centres? And does this countenance 'counterforce' (anti-weapons) capability rather than MAD? Not necessarily: 'counterforce' implies the threat (though not necessarily the intention) of first-strike, since there is little point in knocking out the enemy's weapons silos once the weapons have been fired. NATO continues to reject a 'no first use' policy (one which the Russians, incidentally, have adopted) but the Pastoral states firmly that 'We do not perceive any situation in which the deliberate initiation of nuclear warfare, on however restricted a scale, can be morally justified. Non-nuclear attacks by another state must be resisted by other than nuclear means.' As for the duty of civilians: 'As a people we must refuse to legitimate the idea of nuclear war.'[12]

Such unequivocal guidance from the hierarchy of course created a furore. The White House was appalled. Prominent Catholics within the Reagan Administration did their best to discredit the Bishops. John Lehman Jr., the Navy Secretary, wrote an article in the *Wall Street Journal* arguing that 'If adopted, such recommendations could lead directly to immoral consequences.' William Clark, the then National Security Adviser, also a Catholic, wrote to the Bishops on behalf of the Administration, contending that the Pastoral 'continues to reflect a fundamental misreading of American policies and continues essentially to ignore the far-reaching American proposals that are currently being negotiated with the Soviet Union. . .'[13] Others tried simply to discredit the Bishops: 'Over their heads in a subject they don't understand,' commented one conservative patronisingly.'[14] The hope of the Administration was that the Pope would denounce the Pastoral; but far from doing so, he elevated Bishop Joseph Bernardin of Chicago, the chairman of the commission which first investigated nuclear issues for the Bishop's Conference, to Cardinal in 1983 – hardly a sign of displeasure.

Even within the liberal wing of the Church, there was a recognition that the Pastoral posed great problems: 'To force believers into making a choice creates the potential for the greatest religio-political clash in US history,' commented the editor of the liberal *National Catholic Reporter*.[15]

Within the anti-nuclear movement generally, the Pastoral Letter was welcomed as an enormous step forward. Catholics are the largest single denomination in the United States, and, if united, can wield huge political clout. But even here there were certain reservations. Many of the same people who deeply welcome the Pastoral Letter are less than enthusiastic about Catholic political activism in other fields, such as abortion. Some members of the Catholic hierarchy are not slow to make the same connection. Commenting on the huge anti-nuclear demonstrations in the Federal Republic of Germany at Easter, 1986, the Chairman of the German Catholic Bishops' Conference, Cardinal Joseph Hoeffner, preached in Cologne Cathedral that it was 'a contradiction to protest against rockets and nuclear energy and to keep silent about abortion.'[16] Meanwhile, not long after the American Bishops' Pastoral was finally published, the Papal Nuncio in Europe made a determined effort to get Monsignor Bruce Kent, the Catholic priest who had for many years been Chairman of British CND, reprimanded and removed from this office by his archbishop, Cardinal Basil Hume. He did not succeed. And at the time of writing, Archbishop Raymond Hunthausen of Seattle, one of the radical signatories of the Pastoral letter, has been given a more orthodox 'shadow' to make sure he no longer steps too far out of line. It is clear that, whichever side they take in this particular debate, Catholics will be able to claim high-placed support within the Church.

But if the Catholics are split, so too are the Protestants. While some Catholics distance themselves from a newly respectable radical pacifism, many Protestants are appalled at the spread of the radicalism traditional to nonconformists.

A particularly poignant instance of this is the Anglican Church. When CND was formed, its first Chairman was Canon John Collins of St Paul's Cathedral, but he, like all the other Anglican clergymen involved, was acting as an individual: the Church took no official position on the issue. But when the issue revived in 1979, so many Church members felt strongly about it that this detachment could not be maintained. A working party was convened under the Bishop of Salisbury to study the question of nuclear weapons and strategy and their implications for members of the Church. In particular, they considered the position with regard to British nuclear weapons. The group was not particularly radical. Its chairman, John Austin Baker, spent nineteen years in academic theology before moving to a canonry at Westminster Abbey, where he was also Chaplain to the Speaker of the House of Commons; in 1982, he became Bishop of Salisbury. A more 'establishment' pedigree it would be hard to imagine. The report, however, when it appeared in 1983, was unequivocal. It concluded: 'In the marginal possibility of Britain's having to "go it alone" in defending itself against aggression, would not the lack of an independent British deterrent mean that it had no means of upholding the cause of right – and is that not ethically unacceptable? This is the heart of the matter, the sword that divides. We shall have failed wholly in our presentation if we have not made it clear that in our view the cause of right cannot be upheld by fighting a nuclear war, not only because of the nature of the evil inflicted but also because by destroying one's own society it makes it impossible to preserve the ideals of justice where alone they can exist, in the human community and the individual soul.'[17] Thus the working party came out in favour of Britain renouncing her independent deterrent – or in other words, unilateral nuclear disarmament. American nuclear weapons, it concluded, should also be withdrawn from Britain.

Many members of the Church of England General Synod, to which this report was presented, were exhilarated by it: but many more were appalled. That the Church of England should adopt unilateralism as its official policy was to them unthinkable. 'Unilateralism' is one of those buzz-words which implies a good deal more than it baldly means. In the mouths of the kind of people who traditionally make up the General Synod of the Church of England it could be taken to imply rashness, lack of patriotism, a thoughtless impulsiveness which, if not necessarily of the far left, is knowingly or unknowingly influenced by it. 'Unilateralist' is used dismissively, almost as a smear: right-thinking people are 'multilateralists' (and always have been: already in the early 1960s CND found it necessary to publish a pamphlet explaining that the unilateralist position did not mean that the Russians would be welcomed to Britain with open arms, nor did it mean that unilateralists were against nuclear arms reductions on all sides.) 1983 was an election year in Britain. Michael Heseltine, the Minister of Defence, was mounting a special campaign to discredit CND, whose membership was larger than that of any of the political parties: his special phrase to discredit this dangerous tendency was 'one-sided disarmament' – implying all the worst about unilateralism and leaving out the 'nuclear'. John Selwyn Gummer, the then Chairman of the Conservative Party, was a prominent member of the Synod. It was unthinkable that the report should be adopted, and it was not. (The working party's recommendations have now been officially adopted as Labour Party policy, and are now described by the Prime Minister, Mrs Thatcher, as 'giving the Russians everything they want without even firing a shot.')

The new British Conservative Party presents itself as the party of morals: the new Right are their especial guardians against the depredations of vicious and unthinking sixties liberalism, now defeated. But in the nuclear argument they find themselves on the moral defensive. Here, for example, is the plaint of some members of the right-wing Institute for European Defence Studies: 'E. P. Thompson, the Chairman of European Nuclear Disarmament and the most prominent British intellectual in the campaign for unilateralism, . . . has written that the arguments in favour of the deterrent "stink of mendacious rhetoric". He seldom suggests that those who favour the position of nuclear weapons for the purpose of deterrence might simply be mistaken; in fact they are often depicted as morally deficient or weak; politicians who argue in favour of the Western nuclear deterrent are a particular target of abuse, being characterised as reckless in their policies and dishonest in their public statements. In CND literature and speeches by prominent campaigners the possession of the nuclear weapon is variously described as "criminal", "morally outrageous", "an outrage against humanity", "a moral monstrosity", and "morally imbecilic". In short, it conveys the impression that the unilateralist has a monopoly of virtue.'[18] And now the dread unilateralism had almost officially penetrated one of conservatism's very fortresses, the Church of England! Theology was met with theology: 'Many Christians who have joined [the peace] movement have simply accepted the language and mythology of rationalist radicalism. In particular, they have accepted the optimism typical of that tradition of political thought. They advocate one-sided nuclear disarmament in the belief that, by the force of emulation, it will automatically produce universal disarmament, just as they advocate passive resistance in the belief that it will immobilize the aggressor. Whatever construction may be put on Christ's teaching on these matters, it contains no traces of such optimism. Those enjoined to turn the other cheek were given no expectation that it would not be struck, and those urged by St Paul to do good to their enemies were offered as their reward the assurance that by so doing they would be heaping "coals of fire" on the heads of those enemies, a prospect which, incidentally, cannot have much appeal to humanitarian pacifists. The Christian pacifist movement must therefore be considered part of the general peace movement which has been a recurrent phenomenon in [Britain's] politics for two hundred years and which derives its inspiration from political radicalism. . .'[19]

There is nothing the British Protestant right hates more than

148

fanaticism. The same, in this as in any other aspect of life, is not true of America.

For in America, too, there is a Protestant backlash against traditional nonconformist liberal activism. In Holland and Germany the Church is central to most people's lives, and central also to reform. In Britain, it is for most people more or less an irrelevance: its weight is largely symbolic. But in America it is deeply entwined in every aspect of life, including politics – almost everything in American life, as we have seen, being in some form political. And if the American right sees itself as being locked in combat with the demon Marxism, for the sunbelt fundamentalists who increasingly dominate the American political scene this is nothing less than a holy war.

There is nothing new about this. These are the same demons that obsessed the McCarthyites whose rise was so intimately connected with the history of the atom bomb. When the Alger Hiss trial took place in 1950, Alistair Cooke, in the introduction to his book about it, says that 'It was written during something very like a seventeenth-century religious war.'[20] If people have been driven to protest against nuclear weapons largely on moral grounds, there has been moral fervour – albeit differently based – behind their making and support as well. In 1949, when, after the explosion of the first Soviet bomb, the General Advisory Committee met to consider the question of whether or not to pursue the 'super', Lewis Strauss, one of the Atomic Energy Commissioners, wanted to go on with it because 'a government of atheists is not likely to be dissuaded from producing the weapon on "moral" grounds.'[21]

The same distinction between 'moral' and 'immoral' governments was drawn eight years later by the pious John Foster Dulles. Speaking to the United Nations General Assembly about America's intention to continue nuclear weapons testing, his theme was the moral rightness of the American tests and the immorality of the Soviet Union in opposing them: 'We seek, by experiments now carefully controlled, to find how to eliminate the hazardous radioactive material now incident to the explosions of thermonuclear weapons. Also we seek to make nuclear weapons into discriminating weapons. . . The Soviet Union seems not to want the character of nuclear weapons thus to be refined and changed. It seems to like it that nuclear weapons can be stigmatized as "horror" weapons. Does it calculate that, under these conditions, governments subject to moral and religious influences will not be apt to use them? And would the Soviet Government, not itself subject to moral and religious constraints, thereby gain a special freedom of action and initiative as regards such weapons. . .?'[22]

This sense of being engaged in a holy war and of being imbued with moral rightness has no whit abated since then. Addressing the House Armed Services Committee – a highly conservative body, but nevertheless alarmed by President Reagan's decision to abrogate the Salt II treaty – Richard Perle, the hawkish Assistant Secretary of Defence, said that 'Either the Congress will stand with the Administration . . . or the Congress will stand with the Soviets.'[23] (This classification did little to change the Committee's mind.) President Reagan, himself a born-again fundamentalist, loathes communism and all its works. Speaking of the 'evil empire' he said, 'Here is a direct teaching of the child from the beginning of its life that it is a human being whose only importance is its contribution to the state – that they are wards of the state – that they exist only for that purpose, and that there is no god, they are just an accident of nature. The result is, this is why they have no respect for human life, for the dignity of an individual.'[24]

There are many reasons why such attitudes in people holding great power are frightening. One is that religious missionary fervour is added to the dislike and fear anyway felt by the capitalist for the communist. As the Islamic resurgence shows, there are few things more dangerous than zeal of this kind allied to modern weaponry. Another is something peculiar to Christian fundamentalism: the notion that this 'vale of tears' is merely an irksome preliminary to the realities of heavenly bliss. The effect of this philosophy is to reduce the importance of what happens here on earth: hence, of course, the appeal of fundamentalism to the poor and downtrodden. Not surprisingly, many believers look forward to Armageddon, the last battle which will signal their release. They look forward to it in the most literal terms: for example, two young Jehovah's Witnesses, recently married, once told me they were not planning to have any children until after Armageddon. In a nuclear world this is possibly the most terrifying of all points of view. In restrained Britain it leads to the attitude of the person who wrote to an impassioned anti-nuclear campaigner: 'May I point out that the reason why a number of us, who would otherwise support an anti-nuclear campaign, remain aloof from it is because we feel that the prospect of a nuclear holocaust possesses, for all its horror, an apocalyptic quality of condign retribution.'[25] In cruder American terms it leads to the bumper-sticker associated with the followers of the Reverend Jerry Falwell: IN THE EVENT OF THE RAPTURE THIS CAR WILL BECOME UNMANNED. (This refers to the belief that, just before Armageddon, all true believers will be 'raptured' up to Heaven.)

It would be nice to think that these attitudes and beliefs were confined to a bunch of crackpots well away from the seats of power. But they are not. They command immense and increasing support throughout the United States, starting with the Southern Bible Belt whose attitudes and politicians more and more dominate the American scene, and spreading, by means of national television shows, all over the country. The preachers who sponsor and appear on the TV shows, men like Jerry Falwell, Pat Robertson, Jim Bakker, are rich and powerful: they have access to both the minds and the pockets of millions of Americans. Falwell is an adviser and confidant of President Reagan. Pat Robertson is a serious contender for the next Republican Presidential nomination. They command millions of votes: no politician can afford to ignore them.

It has been pointed out that the history of United States Church involvement in politics suggests that any Administration will ultimately have to respond to religious pressure, as happened with Abolition, Prohibition, civil rights, Vietnam.[26] The man who wrote that had in mind the Catholic Bishops' Pastoral Letter, and clearly imagined that the pressure for nuclear disarmament would ultimately become irresistible. But religious pressure this time is working both ways, and there is no guarantee that in this battle the angels will prevail.

151

Conclusion

It is quite clear that, despite being reviled by 'conventional' politicians, the anti-nuclear movements which have grown up around the world since 1979 have significantly influenced the direction of world politics. They have shifted the base from which the debate begins. No one has less wish to change the current basis of the power blocs nor the direction of the arms buildup than President Reagan (unless it be Mrs Thatcher), but even he was forced from the beginning of his Presidency to make verbal obeisances in the direction of arms control, such was the thrust of world opinion in that direction. And despite everything – despite the appointment of such nuclear super-hawks as Assistant Secretary of Defense Richard Perle to oversee the arms-controllers and make sure they did not get out of hand and the placement of the gung-ho Kenneth Adelman to head up and, hopefully, nullify the Arms Control and Disarmament Agency – the tide seems to be rolling against ever-increasing amounts of ever more complex nuclear armaments.

This has become true because of the advent of Mr Gorbachev at the head of the Soviet Praesidium. Whether because he wishes to free the Soviet economy from the strait-jacket of the nuclear arms race or because he is truly afraid of its consequences, it is clear that one of his main political initiatives is directed towards negotiating nuclear arms reductions. What the peace movement has done is to make it increasingly difficult for such efforts in this direction as the long Soviet moratorium on nuclear weapons tests, or the continuing stream of offers of arms reduction talks with less and less strings attached, to be dismissed out of hand as propaganda exercises and ignored. However reluctantly, Reagan has been forced to substantiate his words with actions. At the time of writing, the parallel between the political atmosphere in 1963, just before the negotiation of the Partial Test-Ban Treaty, seems very great. It is obvious that, given the political will, something real can be achieved – and it is clear that, should this come about, enormous political credit will redound to President Reagan. Some might feel that it is hard to imagine a greater irony. (This irony is not lost on conservatives, either. General Brent Scowcroft, writing about the excitement over 'zero option' proposals in Europe in 1987, admitted that the original 1981 proposal had been made by the United States in the certainty that the Soviet Union would say no. As this could no longer be relied on, the General concluded that it would be unwise to make such a proposal again. Henry Kissinger concluded a recent article with advice to 'be thoughtful about what you propose. The other side may accept it.'[1])

The most likely candidates for the first round of cuts, should any come about – and it must be remembered that nobody has ever yet succeeded in negotiating any actual reductions in nuclear weapons – are those weapons known as the 'INF' – Intermediate Nuclear Forces. These are those very weapons – Cruise, Pershing IIs, SS20s – whose planning and placement brought the anti-nuclear movement back to life. Their removal would be very popular with the European public. Everybody in Western Europe would naturally feel safer without SS20s pointing at them, and a recent opinion poll showed that most Europeans – from 56% of British (the lowest percentage) to 78% of Italians, disapprove of the placement of American nuclear weapons in Europe.[2]

There can be little doubt that this remarkable unanimity results from that debate and discussion which has been forced by the peace movement upon a reluctant NATO ever since these weapons were first mooted. But would their removal (should it come about) mean the end of the European peace movement? It seems clear that it would not. For one thing, the present negotiations are concerned only with land-based weapons and – even should these be removed – it is by no means sure that this would mean weapons reductions. The mood in NATO at the time of writing is merely to replace them with sea- and air-launched missiles. In this case the peace movement would find itself faced both with the new weapons and also with a public sense of false security resulting from a perception that weapons have been reduced when in fact they have not. As one sympathiser remarked to me, 'Well, CND can pack up and go home now, can't it?'

But even should any real reductions take place in intermediate weapons, their removal would precipitate discussion of another question very much at the centre of everyone's mind: namely the future of NATO and the Warsaw Pact.

It is the dear wish of large sections of the peace movement throughout Europe to see a non-nuclear Europe signifying the end of those blocs which so artificially divide it. But even the most conventional European politicians are now looking beyond NATO. Their vision is of a Western European defence union, the WEU. This might disengage Europe from America, but in the eyes of those looking beyond the blocs, would do little more. Yet even here the effects of anti-nuclear sentiment may be seen. Discussing the WEU, Sir Geoffrey Howe, the British Foreign Secretary, noted that 'Within both Britain and West Germany there was no longer political agreement on the role of nuclear weapons in defence policy. It would be prudent for Western Europe to "prepare for the possibility, in the longer run, of a less nuclear world." '[3]

What this seems to indicate is that, far from the peace movement being out on some kind of lunatic limb, its thinking is really only a few years ahead of even conservative politicians (and not at all ahead of that of Mr Gorbachev). Why, then, is it still so continuously reviled?

A clue may perhaps be seen in the success of the anti-apartheid movement in forcing Barclay's Bank to pull out of South Africa despite the British government's reluctance to impose economic sanctions. Increasingly in a small world people feel strongly about issues that transcend national frontiers. Indeed, in today's world details of national policy look increasingly parochial, of importance only to the few people they affect. The significant issues are bigger than that, and they, increasingly, are the subject of single-issue campaigns. The object of such campaigns is, as often as not, to mobilise public opinion in order to force a supranational stance on politicians despite themselves – and to outweigh the 'normal' political channels if need be. Naturally this evokes dislike and distrust among politicians.

Douglas Hurd, the British Home Secretary, was recently quoted as likening pressure-groups to 'sea-serpents, strangling honest Ministers in their coils and distorting the constitutional relationship between Government and electorate.'4 But no pressure group will carry any weight that does not have a large body of opinion behind it. Why should such opinion only be taken into account if it happens to square with the policies of a national government temporarily in power? The fact is that the issues giving rise to such pressure groups often transcend party political lines – as the anti-apartheid and anti-nuclear movements show. It may be that in an ever-smaller world international single-issue campaigns will be an important part of the political future. They are not going to disappear, even though today's politicians may devoutly wish they would.

Notes

CHAPTER 1: A FAILED INFANTICIDE

1) Anthony West, *H.G. Wells, Aspects of a Life*, London, 1954, p. 131.
2) Robert Jungk, *Brighter than a Thousand Suns*, p. 108.
3) Joseph Rotblat: 'Leaving the bomb project.' *Bulletin of the Atomic Scientists*, August 1985, pp. 16–19,
4) Ibid.
5) *In the Matter of J. Robert Oppenheimer*, p. 80.
6) R. Clark, *Einstein*, p. 543.
7) Rotblat, op. cit.
8) Martin J. Sherwin, *A World Destroyed*, p. 284.
9) Clark, op. cit., p. 541.
10) Peierls, 'Reflections of a British participant', *Bulletin of the Atomic Scientists*, August 1985.
11) Ibid.
12) Quoted Rufus E. Miles, Jr., 'Hiroshima: The Strange Myth of Half a Million Lives Saved', *International Security*, Fall 1985, pp. 121–140.
13) Ibid. – from Winston S. Churchill, *The Second World War*, vol. 6, Triumph and Tragedy.
14) Alperovitz, 'More on Atomic Diplomacy', *Bulletin of the Atomic Scientists*, December 1985, pp. 35–7.
15) Miles, op. cit., pp. 136–8.

CHAPTER 2: AMATEURS AND PROFESSIONALS

1) The Franck Report, reproduced Kimball Smith, *A Peril and a hope*, p. 561.

2) Abba P. Lerner, in an article written soon after Hiroshima but not published until the April/May 1947 issue of the *Bulletin of the Atomic Scientists*.
3) General H. H. Arnold, 'The Air Force in the Atomic Age', in Masters *One World or None*, p. 31.
4) Quoted Kimball Smith, op. cit., pp. 80–81.
5) Ibid., p. 89.
6) Groves, *Now It Can Be Told*, p. 410.
7) Norbert Wiener, 'A Scientist Rebels', *Atlantic Monthly*, December 1946.
8) Kimball Smith, op. cit., p. 132.
9) 'The Bulletin and the Scientists' Movement,' *Bulletin of the Atomic Scientists*, December 1985, pp. 19–27.
10) J. D. Bernal, *Science Against War*, London, 1949.
11) David Lilienthal, *Journals: The Atomic Energy Years 1945–1950*, pp. 390–1.
12) E. Snow, *Journey to the Beginning*, quoted Alperovitz, *Atomic Diplomacy*, preface.
13) Irving Langmuir in Masters, *One World or None*, p. 50.
14) Holloway, *The Soviet Union and the Arms Race*, p19.
15) Holloway, Ibid., pp. 15–20.
16) Lilienthal, op. cit., pp. 568–9.

CHAPTER 3: UNDER THE COUNTER

1) *Bulletin of Atomic Scientists*, February 1947.
2) Margaret Gowing, *Britain and Atomic Energy, 1939–1945*.
3) Ibid., p. 212.
4) Ibid., p. 133.
5) John Kennedy and Charles Macleod, *Modern Quarterly*, vol. 5.
6) C. Wright Mills, *The Causes of World War III*, pp. 54–5.
7) R. Clark, *J.B.S.*, p. 189.
8) I. F. Stone, *The Truman Era*, pp. 136–7.
9) Clark, *The Life of Bertrand Russell*, p. 518.
10) Ibid., p. 523.
11) Ibid., p. 526.
12) Ibid., pp. 528–9.
13) Lilienthal, *Change, Hope and the Bomb*, p. 33.
14) I. F. Stone, 'National Suicide as a Form of Defense', *The Haunted Fifties*, p. 119.
15) Cabinet papers, quoted in the *Guardian*, 2 January 1985.
16) Richard Crossman, *Backbench Diaries*, London, 1981, pp. 388–9.

CHAPTER 4: PROTEST

1) The inhabitants of St George are now suffering the effects of living where they do. Almost every family now has a member suffering from some form of cancer.
2) Tame and Robotham, *Maralinga,* p. 197.
3) Duncan Sandys admitted this in his 1957 Defence White Paper.
4) Hugh Brock, 'Marching to Aldermaston – Ten Years Ago?' *Sanity, Aldermaston Daily*, Good Friday 1962.
5) Clark, *Life of Bertrand Russell*, p. 536.
6) Ibid., p. 539.
7) Ibid., p. 540.
8) For a full discussion of the genesis of Pugwash, see Clark, op. cit., pp. 542–5.
9) *Royal United Services Journal*, November 1956.
10) Stone, 'National Suicide as a Form of Defense,' *The Haunted Fifties*, pp. 120–1.
11) Ibid.
12) Miss G. E. M. Anscombe, *President Truman's Degree*, Oxford, 1956.

CHAPTER 5: CND

1) J. B. Priestley, 'Britain and the Nuclear Bombs', *New Statesman*, November 1957.
2) Clark, *Life of Bertrand Russell*, p. 556.
3) This was reprinted in *Sanity*, October 1984, pp. 30–33.
4) Clark, op. cit., p. 557.
5) Ibid.
6) John Humphrey – personal communication with the author.
7) Bolsover and Minnion, *The CND Story*, p. 17.
8) D. Boulton (ed.), *Voices from the Crowd*, London, 1964, p. 59.
9) Priestley, 'Britain and the Nuclear Bombs'.
10) Barbara Deming, *Revolution and Equilibrium*, p. 86, 'Letter to Amitai Etzioni'.
11) Ibid.
12) *The Times*, 14 December 1962.
13) Driver, *The Disarmers*, pp. 232–3.
14) Crossman, *Backbench Diaries*, p. 681.
15) Details from Bolsover and Minnion, op. cit., introduction, pp. 15–16.
16) Crossman, op. cit., p. 681.
17) Quoted Parkin, *Middle Class Radicals*, p. 116n.

CHAPTER 6: ON THE MARCH

1) Haldane, 'The Duties of a Citizen in a Criminal State,' 1938 – from *Keeping Cool*, London, 1940.
2) Driver, op. cit., p. 99.
3) Clark, *Life of Bertrand Russell*, p. 252.
4) *Peace News*, 15 September 1961.
5) NCCL Report: *Public Order and the Police – report on the events in Trafalgar Square, Sunday 17 – Monday 18 September 1961.*
6) Quoted *Peace News*, 9 November 1962.
7) *Guardian*, 14 January 1963.

CHAPTER 7: FALLOUT

1) Gowing, *Britain and Atomic Energy 1939–45,* p. 388n.
2) Quoted Barton J. Bernstein, 'Nuclear Deception: the US record', *Bulletin of the Atomic Scientists*, August/September 1986, pp. 40–45.
3) Freeman Dyson, *Disturbing the Universe*, p. 134.
4) *Observer*, 19 November 1961.
5) Dyson, op. cit., p. 140.
6) *Bulletin of the Atomic Scientists*, September 1959.

CHAPTER 8: THE SIXTIES

1) E. U. Condon, 'Time to Stop Baiting Scientists', *Bulletin of the Atomic Scientists*, February 1958, pp. 80–2.
2) B. Russell, *Has Man a Future?* pp. 71–3.
3) L. Pauling, *No More War!* p. 170.
4) Ibid., pp. 174–5.
5) Harry S. Kalman, 'Sourwine in New Bottles', *Bulletin of the Atomic Scientists*, 1961.
6) A. Herzog, *The War-Peace Establishment*, pp. 114–5.
7) Russell, preface to *Common Sense and Nuclear Warfare*, London, 1959.
8) Herzog, op. cit., p. 238.
9) Ibid.
10) Deming, op. cit., pp. 136–186, 'Letter to WISP'.
11) Quoted *Guardian*, 18 January 1963.
12) Deming, op. cit., p. 141.
13) Ibid., p. 142.

CHAPTER 9: WAGING PEACE

1) R. Fischer and C. Pustan, 'Peace March to Moscow', *British/Soviet Newsletter*, 14 April 1962.
2) Ibid.
3) Deming, op. cit., pp. 114–5.
4) Polly Toynbee, *Guardian*, 17 December 1985.
5) Deming, op. cit., pp. 188–9.
6) Ibid.
7) F. Watson, *The Trial of Mr Gandhi*, London, 1969, p. 159.
8) Deming, op. cit., pp. 36–7.
9) Ibid., p. 30.
10) Ibid.
11) Ibid., pp. 228–9.

CHAPTER 10: ATOMS FOR PEACE

1) Lilienthal, *Atomic Energy Years*, pp. 473–4.
2) Abba P. Lerner, 'The President Addresses the World', *Bulletin of the Atomic Scientists*, April/May 1947.
3) *Too Hot to Handle – Interim Report on the Under-Insurance of British Nuclear Reactors*, Greenpeace, London, 1986, p. 7.
4) Ibid., p. 9.
5) Ibid.
6) Ibid.
7) *Guardian*, 9 July 1985.
8) Richard Burt, *New York Times*, 16 September 1980, quoted David Lowry, *Military spin-offs from civil nuclear programmes: the curious history of the origins of the British Magnox Nuclear Reactor Programme*, p. 2.
9) Frank Barnaby, *Guardian*, 10 September 1981, quoted Lowry, p. 2.
10) R. V. Hesketh, Evidence to the Sizewell Inquiry, *Nuclear Power UK, Nuclear Weapons USA*, 1984.
11) *Hansard*, 9 May 1959, col. 64, quoted Lowry, p. 27.
12) Quoted Lowry, p. 30.
13) Ibid., p. 30a.
14) Ibid., note 33.
15) Hesketh, op. cit., pp. 65–6.
16) Ibid., p. 66.
17) Lowry, op.cit., pp. 42, 46.
18) Lowry: *Reflections on Britain's Nuclear History: A Conversation with Lord Hinton*, Open University, Energy Research Group, 1984, pp. 36–7.

160

CHAPTER 11: PROTEST RESURFACES

1) See Papadakis, *The Green Movement in West Germany*, pp. 65–8.
2) Ibid., p. 69.
3) Ibid., p. 70
4) Ibid., p. 70–1.
5) Ibid., pp. 20–1.
6) In the opinion of Clive Ponting, an ex-senior civil servant at the Ministry of Defence.
7) Diane Johnstone, *The Politics of Euromissiles*, pp. 109–10.
8) *Der Spiegel*, 1 February 1981, quoted Bertell, *No Immediate Danger*, p. 280.
9) Johnstone, op. cit., p. 94.
10) Ibid., pp. 94–5.
11) Bob Overy, *How Effective Are Peace Movements?*

CHAPTER 12: AMERICA AND THE FREEZE

1) Christopher Paine, 'Lobbying for Arms Control', *Bulletin of the Atomic Scientists*, August, 1985.
2) Ibid.
3) *World Military and Social Expenditure 1982*. Quoted Dave Elliott, *Defence Industry Conversions: A Review of Options*, Open University Alternative Technology Group, Milton Keynes, 1985.
4) Alexander Cockburn and James Ridgway, 'The Freeze', *New Left Review*, January/February 1983, p. 11.
5) Stan Pressman, 'Nuclear Freeze Groups Focus on Candidates', *Congressional Quarterly*, 5 May 1984, p. 1024.
6) Ibid.
7) Cockburn and Ridgeway, p. 20.

CHAPTER 13: TRIGGERPOINTS

1) Rip Bulkeley, letter to the *Guardian*, 23 March 1985.
2) Lynne Jones, 'Changing Ideas of Authority', *New Statesman*, 23 November 1984.
3) *Observer*, 28 October 1962.
4) Deming, op cit., p. 117
5) Richard L. Zweigenhaft, 'Students surveyed about Nuclear War', *Bulletin of the Atomic Scientists*, February 1985, pp. 26–7.
6) *London Under Attack* – report of the Greater London Area War Risk Study, Oxford, 1986, Appendix 5.

7) Janis and Terwilliger, 'An Experimental Study of Psychological Resistances to Fear Arousing Communications', *Journal of Abnormal and Social Psychology*, 1962, vol. 65, no. 6, pp. 403–10.

8) E. P. Thompson, 'The Doomsday Consensus', *Writing by Candlelight*, p. 275.

9) Schell, *The Fate of the Earth*, p. 3.

10) Ibid., p. 113.

11) Ibid., p. 226.

12 C. Wright Mills, *The Causes of World War Three*. p. 44

13) Ibid., p. 173.

CHAPTER 14: SECRETS

1) Lilienthal, *Atomic Energy Years*, p. 10.

2) Ibid., pp. 11–12.

3) Heclo and Wildavsky, *The Private Government of Public Money*, p. 80.

4) *Observer*, 26 May 1985.

5) *Guardian*, 23 March 1987.

6) Gowing, *Independence and Deterrence*, vol.1, p. 52.

7) Barbara Castle, *The Castle Diaries*: 1964–70, London, 1984, p. 306.

8) Morton Halperin, 'Secrecy and National Security', *Bulletin of the Atomic Scientists*, August 1985.

9) Ibid.

10) Aldous Huxley, *The Politics of Ecology*, 1963, Occasional Paper for the Center for the Study of Democratic Institutions, Santa Barbara, California.

11) Letter to Jacquetta Hawkes, quoted Driver, *The Disarmers,* p. 187.

12) Philip Steadman, 'The Bomb: worse than government admits', *New Scientist*, 18 June 1981, pp. 169–71.

13) British Medical Association: *Report of the Board of Science and Education Inquiry into the Medical Effects of Nuclear War*, March 1983.

14) *E. N. D. Journal*, Summer 1985, p. 5.

15) Karen Lewton, 'Watching You Watching Me', *Sanity* August 1986, pp. 12–15.

16) Ibid.

17) Ibid.

CHAPTER 15: WHY DO PEOPLE HATE THE PEACE MOVEMENT?

1) *Guardian*, 7 February 1985.

2) Caroline Blackwood, *On The Perimeter*, pp. 70–71.

3) Ibid., p. 98.
4) Cockburn and Ridgway, 'The Freeze', *New Left Review*, February 1983.
5) *Guardian*, 17 November 1986.
6) Angelo Codevilla, *NATO Today: Curing Self-Inflicted Wounds*, Institute for European Defence Studies, 1984.

CHAPTER 16: RELIGIOUS WAR AND RELIGIOUS PEACE

1) Crossman, *Backbench Diaries*, pp. 821–2.
2) Scheer, *With Enough Shovels*, p. 96.
3) *Friend*, 14 September 1962, quoted Driver, *The Disarmers*, p. 67.
4) *The Church and the Bomb: nuclear weapons and Christian conscience*, p. 159.
5) 'Anti-Politics and Successor Generations', *Journal of Political and Military Sociology*, pp. 177–181.
6) C. Bruce Van Voorst, 'The Churches and Nuclear Deterrence', *Foreign Affairs* 61, pp. 827–52.
7) *Guardian*, 6 April, 1985.
8) Van Voorst, p. 832.
9) I. F. Stone, *The Hidden History of the Korean War*, pp. 92–3.
10) I. F. Stone, *The Haunted Fifties*, p. 83: 'The Oppenheimer Verdict'.
11) Van Voorst, op. cit., p. 832.
12) Ibid., pp. 834–7.
13) Ibid., p. 846.
14) Phyllis Shlafly, quoted ibid., p. 849.
15) Ibid., p. 850.
16) *Guardian*, 31 March 1986.
17) *The Church and the Bomb*, p. 162.
18) Towle et al., *Protest and Perish*, 1983.
19) T. E. Utley, *British Churches and the Peace Movement*, Institute of European Defence Studies, 1983.
20) Cooke, *A Generation on Trial*, 1950.
21) Letter to Truman, 25 November 1949, quoted H. York, *The Advisors*, p. 59.
22) Speech to UN General Assembly, 19 September 1957.
23) *Guardian*, 7 June 1986.
24) Scheer, op. cit., p. 42.
25) Letter to Nicholas Humphrey, 20 December 1981.
26) Van Voorst, op. cit.

CONCLUSION

1) Quoted by Christopher Hitchens, *New Statesman*, 10 April 1987, p. 16.

2) *Guardian*, 16 February 1987.
3) *Guardian*, 17 March 1987.
4) *Observer*, 30 March 1986.

Select Bibliography

Alperovitz, Gar: *Atomic Diplomacy*, London, 1966.
Amrine, Michael: *The Great Decision: the secret history of the Atomic Bomb*, London, 1960.
Baxter, James Finney: *Scientists against Time*, Boston, 1946.
Bertell, Rosalie: *No Immediate Danger*, London, 1985.
Blackett, P.M.S.: *Atomic Weapons and East-West Relations*, Cambridge, 1956.
Blackett, P.M.S.: *The Military and Political Consequences of Atomic Energy*, London, 1948.
Blackwood, Caroline, *On The Perimeter*, London, 1984.
Bolsover, P. and J. Minnion (eds): *The CND Story*, London, 1983.
Borrie, Christopher J., and Alan Platt: *British Nuclear Policymaking*, RAND, 1984.
Brodie, Bernard: *Strategy in the Missile Age*, Princeton, 1965.
Brown, Harrison and James Neal: *Community of Few*, Santa Barbara, 1960.
Bulletin of the Atomic Scientists, 1946.
Chambers, Whittaker: *Witness*, New York, 1953.
Church of England Board for Social Responsibility: *The Church and the Bomb: Nuclear Weapons and Christian conscience*, London, 1982.
Clark, Ronald W.: *Einstein*, London, 1973.
Clark, Ronald W.: *J. B. S: a biography of J. B. S Haldane*, London, 1968.
Clark, Ronald W.: *The Birth of the Bomb*, London, 1961.
Clark, Ronald W.: *The Life of Bertrand Russell*, London, 1975.
Cockburn, Alexander, and James Ridgway: 'The Freeze', *New Left Review* 137, January-February 1983.
Cooke, Alistair: *A Generation on Trial*, London, 1950.

Deming, Barbara: *Revolution and Equilibrium*, New York, 1971.

Driver, Christopher: *The Disarmers*, London, 1964.

Dyson, Freeman: *Disturbing the Universe*, London, 1981.

Dyson, Freeman: *Weapons and Hope*, London, 1984.

Eatherly, Claude, and Gunther Anders: *Burning Conscience*, London, 1963.

Eaton, Peter: *The Role of the Peace Movements in the 1930s: Who Was for Munich?* Pamphlet 1, Univ. Group on Defence Policy, chairman D. V. Glass, London, 1961–2.

Elliott, David: *Defence Industry Conversion: A Review of the Options*, Open University, 1985.

Fermi, Laura: *Atoms in the Family*, London, 1955.

Goudsmit, Samuel A: *Alsos*, New York, 1947.

Gowing, Margaret: *Britain and Atomic Energy, 1939–1945*, London, 1964.

Gowing, Margaret: *Independence and Deterrence*, London, 1974.

Groves, Leslie R: *Now It Can Be Told*, London, 1963.

Harford, Barbara, and Sarah Hopkins (eds): *Greenham Common: Women at the Wire*, London, 1984.

Hersey, John: *Hiroshima*, London, 1946.

Herzog, Arthur: *The War-Peace Establishment*, New York, 1963.

Hesketh, Ross: *Nuclear Power UK, Nuclear Weapons USA*, Evidence to the Sizewell Inquiry, 1984.

Hiebert, E.N.: *The impact of Atomic energy: History of responses by Government, Scientists and Religious Groups*, Kansas, 1961.

Holloway, David: *The Soviet Union and the Arms Race*, London and New Haven 1983.

Howard, Michael: *War and the Liberal Conscience*, London, 1978.

Huie, W. Bradford: *Hiroshima Pilot*, New York, 1964.

Humphrey, Nicholas: *Four Minutes to Midnight*, London, 1982.

Johnstone, Diane: *The Politics of Euromissiles*, London, 1984.

Jungk, Robert: *Brighter than a Thousand Suns – a personal history of the atomic scientists*, London, 1982.

Kahn, Herman: *On Thermonuclear War*, Princeton, 1960.

Kaltfleiter, Werner, and Robert L. Pfaltzgraff, (eds): *The Peace Movements in Europe and the United States*, London, 1985.

Kamen, Martin D.: *Radiant Science, Dark Politics*, London, 1985.

Kaplan, Fred M.: *Dubious Specter*, New York, 1980.

Kennan, George: *Russia, the Atom and the West*, London, 1958.

Kenny, Anthony: *The Logic of Deterrence*, London, 1985.

Liddell Hart, B.H.: *Deterrence or Defence*, London, 1960.

Lief, Alfred (ed.): *The Fight against War*, New York, 1933; Morristown, 1973.

Lifton, Robert J.: *Death in Life: the Survivors of Hiroshima*, New York, 1967.

Lilienthal, David: *Change, Hope and the Bomb*, Princeton, 1963.

Lilienthal, David: *Journals: The Atomic Energy Years*, New York, 1964.

Lovins, Amory: *Energy War*, London, 1982.

Lowry, David: *Military spin-offs from civil nuclear programmes*, Open University, 1986.

Masters, Dexter and Katharine Way (eds): *One World or None – a Report to the Public on the full meaning of the Atomic Bomb*, Chicago, 1946.

Mills, C. Wright: *The Power Elite*, Oxford, 1956.

Mills, C. Wright: *The Causes of World War III*, New York, 1958.

Openshaw, Stan, Philip Steadman and Owen Greene: *Doomsday: Britain After Nuclear Attack*, Oxford, 1983.

Oppenheimer, R: *In the Matter of J. Robert Oppenheimer*, USAEC Transcript of Hearings before the Personnel Security Board, Washington, 1954.

Overy, Bob: *How Effective are Peace Movements?* London, 1980.

Papadakis, Elim: *The Green Movement in West Germany*, London, 1984.

Parkin, Frank: *Middle Class Radicals*, Manchester, 1968.

Pauling, Linus: *No More War*, New York, 1958.

Prins, Gwyn, (ed.): *Defended to Death*, London, 1983.

Rotblat, Joseph: *Pugwash*, Prague, 1967.

Russell, Bertrand: *Democracy and Direct Action*, London, 1919.

Russell, Bertrand: *Has Man a Future?* London, 1961.

Russell, Bertrand: *Russell, Khruschev and Dulles – the vital letters of*: London, 1958.

Scheer, Richard: *With Enough Shovels*, New York, 1982.

Schell, Jonathan: *The Fate of the Earth*, London, 1982.

Sherwin, Martin J: *A World Destroyed: The Atomic Bomb and the Grand Alliance*, New York, 1975.

Smith, Alice Kimball: *A Peril and a Hope: the scientists' movement in America 1945–7*, Chicago, 1965.

Snow, C.P.: *Science and Government*, Harvard, 1960

Stern, Philip M: *The Oppenheimer Case – Security on Trial*, New York, 1964.

Stone, I.F.: *The Truman Era*, London, 1953.

Stone, I.F.: *The Haunted Fifties*, London, 1964.

Stone, I.F.: *The Hidden History of the Korean War*, London 1969.

Stonier, Tom: *Nuclear Disaster*, London, 1964.

Szilard, Leo: Memoir in *The Intellectual Migration*, Harvard, 1969.

Talbott, Strobe: *Deadly Gambits*, London, 1985.

Tame, Adrian and F. P. J. Robotham: *Maralinga: British A-bomb, Australian Legacy*, Sydney, 1982.

Thompson, E.P.: *Writing by Candlelight*, London, 1980.

Thompson, E.P.: *Zero Option*, London, 1982.

Thompson, E.P.: *The Heavy Dancers*, London, 1985.

Thompson, E.P., and Dan Smith (eds): *Protest and Survive*, London, 1980.

Towle, Philip, Ian Elliott and Gerald Frost: *Protest and Perish*, London, 1982.

Walters, Robert E: *The Nuclear Trap*, Harmondsworth, 1974

York, Herbert: *The Advisors: Oppenheimer, Teller and the Superbomb*, New York, 1976.

Zuckerman, Solly: *Nuclear Illusion and Reality*, London, 1982.

Index

Acheson, Dean 15, 17, 41
Adelman, Kenneth 152
Aldermaston protests 31–2, 39, 44, 52
Allison, Samuel K. 12–13
Alperovitz, Gar 8–9
American Friends Service Committee 70, 71, 74
American-Soviet Science Society 62
Anderson, Sir John 54
Anscombe, G. E. M. 36
Arms Control and Disarmament Agency (ACDA) 65, 152
arms race 10, 11, 20, 26, 44
Arnold, Gen. H.H. 11–12
Atlantic Monthly journal 14, 47
atom bomb: development 3–7, 139–40
  effects 8, 20, 28, 35–6, 54–5, 62;
  justification 7–9
Atom Harvest (Bertin) 109–10
atomic energy: peaceful use 7–8, 83–4;
  military control 15; *see also* nuclear energy
Atomic Energy Authority 27, 88
Atomic Energy Bill (1947) 21
Atomic Energy Commission 16, 21, 26, 31, 90–1
Attlee, Clement 27, 38, 43, 54–5, 121
Augstein, Rudolf 51
authority, desanctification 76, 77

Baker, Russell 68
Baruch, Bernard 17, 18, 26
Becker, Hans-Detlev 51
Bernal, J. D. 2, 7–8, 17–18, 30
Berrigan, Daniel 143
Bertin, Leonard 109–10
Bevan, Aneurin 37, 38, 45
biological weapons, ban 34–5
Blackett, P.M.S. 38
Bohr, Niels 2, 6
Born, Max 33–4
Bridgman, Percy W. 33
British Association of Atomic Scientists 23
British Broadcasting Corporation (BBC) 28, 32, 58, 59
British Medical Association (BMA) 129
Brock, Hugh 31
Brooke, Sir Norman 28
Brown, George 45
Bulletin of the Atomic Scientists 18, 56, 64, 93
Byrnes, James F. 9

Calder Hall 87, 88
Callaghan, James 93, 101
Cambridge Scientists' Anti-War Group 2, 37

Campaign for Nuclear Disarmament (CND) 39, 40, 41–3, 44, 46–50, 52–3, 54, 59, 60, 74–5, 97–8, 105, 111, 138
Carson, Rachel 81
Carter, President Jimmy 87, 93
Castle, Barbara 29, 121
Catholics and the bomb 142, 143–6, 151
Central Electricity Generating Board (CEGB) 84, 87–92, 109
Chadwick, James, 4, 5
Chapelcross reactor 88
chemical weapons, ban 34–5
Chernobyl disaster 112
Cherwell, Lord 23
Chevaline warhead 121–2
China, tests 57–8
Christianity and the bomb 140–51
Christmas Island 37, 71
Church, the, and the bomb 140–51
Churchill, Winston S. 6, 8, 18, 27, 28, 54
Citrine, Sir Walter 89
civil defence 37, 52–3, 124–30
civil disobedience 47–50
CND see Campaign for Nuclear Disarmament
CNVR see Committee for Non-Violent Resistance
Cold War 17, 20, 23, 27
Collins, Rev. John 39, 146
Comfort, Alex 40
Committee for Non-Violent Resistance (CNVR) 70–1, 74
Committee of 100, 47, 48–50, 52, 53
Commoner, Barry 63, 82–3
Condon Edward U. 30, 61–2, 82, 122
Conservative Party 27, 43, 45, 98, 101, 114, 121, 125, 147
Cooper, Sir Frank 138
Creech-Jones, Arthur 29
Crossman, Richard 28–9, 41, 43–4, 139
Cruise missiles 75, 93, 98, 101, 111, 140, 141, 153

Cuban missile crisis (1962) 54, 57, 69, 112
Curie, Marie 2

Davidson, Carl 77
defence: civil 37, 52–3, 124–30; non-nuclear 101-2; nuclear 12, 22, 37, 41–2, 51, 52–3, 125
defence spending 23, 106
Deming, Barbara 40–1, 67, 69, 73, 76, 78, 112
democracy, bomb impinging on 118, 131
deterrence 23–4, 53, 126, 137
Direct Action 60
direct mail shots 106–7
D-notices 22
Driver, Christopher 43
Dulles, John Foster 38, 149
Dunning, Gordon 82
Dyson, Freeman 55

East Germany, Church 141–2
Eaton, Cyrus 34
Ecology Party 98
Einstein, Albert 3–4, 33, 34
Einstein-Russell Manifesto (1955) 33–4
Eisenhower, Dwight D. 19, 27, 63, 86
Eklund, Sigvard 87
Electric Boat protest 78, 79
Ellsberg, Daniel 123
environmentalists, pressure 81–3, 85, 86, 95, 103
Etzioni, Amitai 40
Euratom agreement 86
European Federation against Nuclear Arms 60
exorcism, tactic 76

Fallex 62 NATO exercises 50, 52
fall-out 35–6, 54–7, 62, 63, 69, 81, 82
FAS see Federation of Atomic Scientists
Fate of the Earth, The (Schell) 58, 108, 110, 115–16
fear, public 17–18, 54, 69, 99, 112, 114
Federal Republic of Germany see West Germany

Federation of Atomic Scientists (FAS) 13, 15, 18, 21, 41, 64, 105
Feminine Mystique, The (Friedan) 70, 81
Fischer, Regina 72–3
fission 2, 4, 19
Flugge, S. 4
Foot, Michael 44, 47
Forsberg, Randall 104
Fortune magazine 7
France: nuclear power 85, 86; protest, lack of 98–101; tests 57–8
Franck Report (1945) 10–11, 111
Freedom of Information Act (1964) 121, 122–3
Freeman, John 26
Freeze campaign 103, 104–8, 134–5
Friedan, Betty 70, 81
Friends of the Earth 103
Frisch, Otto 2, 7
Fuchs, Klaus 19, 30, 61

Gaitskell, Hugh 44–5, 139
Gandhi, Mahatma 47, 77–8
genetic disease 35–6, 54–7, 62, 82
Germany, atomic bomb 3, 4, 5; *see also* East Germany; West Germany
Goodman, Paul 67, 73, 74, 75, 81
Gorbachev, Mikhail 136, 152, 154
Gore, Albert 107–8
Goudsmit, S. A. 56, 58
Gowing, Margaret 22
Great Britain: atomic bomb 3, 7, 21–3; hydrogen bomb 37; nuclear power industry 84, 85, 87–92, 112; nuclear weapons 98; protest 31–2, 36, 37–40, 41–3, 46–50, 52–3, 97–8, 101–2, 115; secrecy 21–3, 27, 52–3, 119–22, 128–31; tests 109–10; US bases 44; as world leader 40–1
Greene, Sir Hugh 59
Greenham Common 111; women 75–7, 104, 133–4
Green Movement 95–7
Greenwood, Anthony 53
Gromyko, Andrei 18

Groves, Gen. Leslie 5, 7, 12, 13, 55, 118–19
Guadeloupe summit (1979) 93, 101

Hahn, Otto 2, 3, 5
Haldane, J.B.S. 2, 24
Halperin, Morton 122, 123
Hammarskjold, Dag 63
Harriman, Averell 57
'Harry', test 31
Hart, Judith 45
Harwell 23, 24, 31
H-Bomb Campaign Committee (1957) 37
Heseltine, Michael 147
Hesketh, Ross 88–9, 91
Hinton, Lord 91–2
Hiroshima 7, 25
Holland, protest 111–12, 130, 140, 141
Horobin, Sir Ian 91
Howe, Sir Geoffrey 154
HUAC *see* United States, House Un-American Activities Committee
Humphrey, Nick 130–1
Hurd, Douglas 154
Huxley, Aldous 124, 126
hydrogen bomb 25, 26, 27–8, 28–9, 31, 35–6, 61
Hydrogen Bomb National Campaign 37

Infeld, Leopold 33
information, availability 21, 27; *see also* secrecy
insurance 84–5
Intermediate Nuclear Forces (INF) 153
International Atomic Energy Agency 86, 87
international control of nuclear energy 6, 10–11, 17, 18–19, 20, 22, 26
Italy, nuclear power 85

Jakobi, Dr 51
Japan, bombing 7–9
Jeger, George 22

Joliot-Curie, Frederic 30, 32–3
Jones, T. K. 127
Jungk, Robert 95

Kahn, Herman 124, 125, 139
Kamen, Martin 82
Kennan, George 38
Kennedy, President John F. 64–5, 112
Kent, Mons. Bruce 146
Khrushchev, Mrs 73
Khruschchev, Nikita 38
Korean war 143–4
Kurchatov, Igor 20

Labour Party 27, 29, 43–5, 46, 98,
    101–2, 114, 121, 139, 147
Langmuir, Irving 19
Laser Isotope Separation 87
Lemnitzer, Gen. Lyman 65
Lerner, Abba P. 84
Lewis, Fulton 63–4
Lewton, Karen 131
Liberal/SDP Alliance 98
lifestyle politics 66, 67, 73–4, 81
Lilienthal, David 16, 17, 18, 20, 26, 36,
    83, 118–19
Los Alamos (New Mex.) 4, 5–6, 7,
    12–13, 16
Lovett, Robert A. 65
Lovins, Amory 86
Lowry, David 91–2

McCarthy, Joe 30, 61
McCormack, Brig.-Gen. James 20
McMahon, Brien 16
McMahon Act 22, 89
Macmillan, Sir Harold 89
Manhattan Project, The 4, 5–6, 12–13,
    19, 118
Marchais, Georges 99
Marchetti, Victor 123
Marshall, General 9
Marshall, Walter 92
Martin, Kingsley 38
May, Alan Nunn 16, 30
May-Johnson Bill (1945) 11, 13 14, 15,
    16

Meany, George 56
Meitner, Lise 2
military secrecy 11, 12, 13–14, 15
Mills, C. Wright 23–4, 116–17
Mitterrand, François 99
Molesworth peace camp 133
Montebello agreement (1983) 121
Montgomery, Field Marshal 35
Moscow peace walk (1960–61) 72–3
Muller, Hermann J. 33
multilateralists 40
Murray, Thomas E. 35
Mutual Assured Destruction (MAD)
    125
Mutual Defence Agreement (1958)
    89–91
MX missiles 105, 107–8

Nagasaki 7, 13
National Committee for the Abolition
    of Nuclear Weapons Tests 37, 39
National Committee for a Sane Nuclear
    Policy (SANE) 70, 71, 105
National Council for Civil Liberties 49
NATO, nuclear weapons 35, 39, 44,
    50–2, 60, 93, 96, 125, 153
neutron bomb 111–12, 120–1, 140
New Statesman journal 7, 28, 38, 47
New University Thought journal 71
Non-Proliferation Treaty (1968) 86
non-violence 75, 77–80
Normanbrook, Lord 59
Now It Can Be Told (Groves) 13
Nuclear Disaster (Stonier) 58, 110
nuclear energy, civil use 57, 81, 82–90;
    and military use 86, 87–92
nuclear fission 2, 4, 19
Nuclear Information factsheet 82
nuclear winter 110

Official Secrets Acts 52
Okinawa island 8
openness *see* secrecy
Oppenheimer, J. Robert 4, 12, 26, 30,
    55, 61, 139, 144
Orion, Project 57, 58
Orr-Harter, Jan 142–3

Palmer, Arthur 91
Partial Test-Ban Treaty (1963) 34, 54, 55–9, 60, 63, 65, 73, 75, 81, 82
passive resistance 47–50, 75, 77–80
Pauling, Linus 33, 62–4, 82
peace movements *see* protest
Peace Pledge Union 37
Peierls, Rudolf 6–7
Perle, Richard 140, 150, 152
Pershing II missiles 93, 111, 153
Pirie, Antoinette 127
Plowshare, Project 57, 58
plutonium, CEGB 87–92
police and protesters 49–50, 78, 80, 130–1
politics, differing views of 66–7
Posner, Blanche 68–9
Potsdam Conference (1945) 9, 10, 55
Powell, Cecil F. 33
Presbyterians and the bomb 142–3
pressure groups 14, 15, 16, 21, 105–7, 154–5
preventive war 24
Priestley, J. B. 37, 38, 40
protest 30–6, 37–44, 46–53, 58, 60, 62–9, 70–80, 94–102, 103–8; lack of 23–7; maintaining 113–17; reaction to 49–50, 78–80, 130–1, 133–8; triggering 109–13
Protestants and the bomb 141, 146–9
public opinion 27–9, 60, 113–14, 154–5; *see also* pressure groups
Pugwash organisation 34, 62
Pustan, Cyril 72–3

radiation, effects *see* fall-out
Reagan, President Ronald 93, 99, 104–5, 107, 116, 134, 135–6, 150, 152–3
Redgrave, Vanessa 52
Regional Seats of Government (RSG) 52, 53, 126
relativity, theory of 5
religion, and the bomb 140–51
Reston, James 63
Reykjavik summit 135
Roosevelt, President F. D. 3–4, 6

Rotblat, Joseph 4–6, 33, 34
Russell, Bertrand 25–6, 32, 33–4, 38, 39, 40–1, 47–8, 52, 62, 65–7
Russia *see* Soviet Union

Sandys, Duncan 27, 42, 111
SANE *see* National Committee for a Sane Nuclear Policy
San Francisco-Moscow peace walk (1960–61) 72–3
Sanity journal 71, 131
Schell, Jonathan 58, 108, 110, 115–16
Schmidt, Helmut 93, 96
Scientist and Citizen factsheet 82
Scientists Against Nuclear Arms (SANA) 129
scientists: and politics 1–2, 16–17; protest 13, 16–17, 33–4, 63–4, 111; and secrecy 3, 12–18, 30; and security 61–2, 118–19
SDI 15
SDP 98
secrecy 3, 6, 11, 12–18, 21–4, 27–8, 30, 52–3, 110, 118–32
security 61–4, 118–32
shelters 125, 127, 128
Shils, Edward 21
Silent Spring (Carson) 81
'Simon' test 31
single-issue campaigns ix, x, 60, 93, 108, 154, 155
Sizewell enquiry (1983) 88–9, 91–2
Snow, C. P. 22
Soviety Union: atom bomb 11–12, 19–20, 24–5, 30; as enemy 5, 6, 7, 9, 11, 19, 24–5, 135; hydrogen bomb 31; and Japan 9; nuclear power industry 85
Spiegel, Der magazine 50–1, 52, 94
Spies for Peace 52–3, 126
Sputnik 37, 38, 89
Stalin, Joseph 9, 19–20, 25
Starbird, General 90
Star Wars *see* Strategic Defence Initiative
Steadman, Philip 128
Stimson, Harry 8, 9, 15

Stone, I.F. 24, 27, 35
Stonier, Tom 58, 110
Strachey, John 44
Strategic Defence Initiative (SDI) 15
Strauss, Franz-Josef 51, 94
Strauss, George 22
Strauss, Lewis 89–90, 149
strontium 90 35–6, 54–7, 69
Students for a Democratic Society (SDS) 77
Sweden, nuclear power 86–7
Switzerland, civil defence 125
symbolism, importance 75, 76, 77
Szilard, Leo 3, 15

Teller, Edward 26, 57
Templin, Ralph 78
terror *see* fear
tests 31, 37, 44, 55–7, 62, 71, 81, 82, 109–10, 111, 149; ban on 34, 54, 56–9, 60, 63, 65, 73, 75, 81, 82
Thatcher, Margaret 93, 98, 101, 125, 135–6, 147
Thompson, E. P. 115, 148
threat *see* fear
Three Mile Island 85
Tizard, Sir Henry 38
Touraine, Alain 23
Trident 98, 101
Truman, President Harry S. 9, 17, 19, 36, 54, 83
Tube Alloys project 3, 4

underground civil defence 124–5, 126
underground storage 12
underground tests 57
unilateralists 40, 46, 147
United Nations 17, 63
United Nations Association for the United States (UNA) 70, 71
United States: atom bomb 3–9, 11; defence spending 106; House Un-American Activities Committee (HUAC) 61–2, 64, 67–9, 70, 73; as military power 14; nuclear power industry 84–5, 103; Presidential

Directive 59 87; protest 40–1, 60, 62–9, 70–5, 78, 80, 103–8, 115–17, 142–5; public pressure 14, 16, 21, 104–7; secrecy 11, 12, 13–14, 21, 27, 35, 118–19, 122–4; security, fears 61–4, 66, 118–19, 122–4
United World Federalists (UWF) 70–1
uranium, fission 2, 4, 19
Urey, Harold 15

Vance, Commissioner 90–1

Wagner, Richard 120–1
Wallace, Henry 15
War Game, The (TV film) 28, 58–9
Watkins, Peter 28, 58–9
Wells, H. G. 2–3
Western European Union 154
West Germany: Green movement 95–7; nuclear weapons 39, 44, 60, 96; protest 39, 50–2, 94–7, 111–12, 141, 142
Wiener, Norbert 14–15
Willens, Harold 106
WILPF *see* Women's International League for Peace and Freedom
Wilson, Dagmar 67
Wilson, Robert 111
WISP *see* Women Strike for Peace
Women's International League for Peace and Freedom (WILPF) 70, 71, 134
Women Strike for Peace (WISP) 67–9, 70, 71, 73, 134
World Association of Parliamentarians for World Government 33
World Federation of Scientific Workers 32
World Peace Council 30
World Set Free, The (Wells) 2–3
Wyhl protest (1975) 94–5

Yount, Hubert W. 84–5
Yukawa, Hideki 33

Zuckerman, Solly 121